Affinity Publisher
for
Ads and Covers

AFFINITY PUBLISHER FOR
SELF-PUBLISHING

BOOKS 2 AND 3

M.L. HUMPHREY

SELECT TITLES BY M.L. HUMPHREY

CONTENTS

Affinity Publisher for Ad Creatives

AFFINITY PUBLISHER FOR
SELF-PUBLISHING - BOOK 2

M.L. HUMPHREY

CONTENTS

INTRODUCTION

In *Affinity Publisher for Fiction Layouts* I walked readers through how to use Affinity Publisher to create a print layout for a novel, short story collection, or other work of fiction.

Eventually I will also do the same for non-fiction books which require a few additional skills such as the ability to insert images within the text of the document, the creation of tables of contents and an index, as well as combining multiple Affinity files into one book. Those books both share a common approach to Affinity Publisher and are in line with the main expected use of the program.

But because I'm cheap and lazy, I also use Affinity Publisher for the creation of basic book covers as well as my ad creatives for things like Amazon A+ Content and Facebook ads.

In reality, the ideal product for covers is probably Affinity Photo not Publisher because it's the program you'd use for things like photo manipulation, but I'm not a skilled graphic designer so I don't do that with my covers.

For ads, though, Affinity Publisher is a great choice since you're mostly combining existing elements into a new image and that can definitely be done with Publisher.

So that's what we're going to focus on in this book: how to use Affinity Publisher to create ad images.

The examples in this book are going to be for Amazon A+ content, Facebook ads, and BookBub CPC ads, but you can easily apply what we're going to do here to any website graphics. Basically, if you know the dimensions you're working with for an online image, you should be able to create it when you're done with this book.

Specifically, we will cover how to:

- Create a cover image for use in Amazon A+ Content Comparison Chart listings

- Create a combined image with all of your series covers for use in Amazon A+ Content

- Create a square Facebook ad that uses your book cover for the background

- Create a square Facebook ad that uses an image for half of the ad

- Create a BookBub CPC ad image with various image adjustments and a 99 cent label

We will walk through from start to finish how to do each of the above. This means that at times we will repeat certain skills. While each project will be presented on a standalone basis, I'd recommend that you work through the projects in order because we'll be building up your skills as we progress through the book. The first time I present a skill I'll do so in detail, but the next time I present it I'll do so in a much shorter manner.

For example, it's very easy to create the cover image to use in Amazon's A+ Content. Very easy. But that also requires a handful of basic skills that we can cover in a very low-pressure setting before we use them on other projects that are more complex.

Also, once you've gone through the book you can reference the Appendix at the back for a quick refresh on each of the skills we covered if you happen to forget the details of how to do it. That will save having to read through a lot of pages just to find out how to do X.

Now, keep in mind I am not a graphic designer. Nor am I a cover design or advertising professional.

I am a self-taught self-published author who learned these skills because I have little to no patience to wait for others to do things for me. If my Facebook (FB) ad isn't working, I want to change out that image today not three weeks from now when my designer can fit me in and at a cost of $25. (If I'm lucky to have someone that responsive and cheap that I can reach out to.)

What we're going to do here should be accessible to any user willing to put in the time and effort (and maybe do a little math, but not much), but don't expect to be some sort of high-level design guru when we're done. If there are special secrets out there, I don't know them.

I will also add that I absolutely believe every self-published author should master the basics of what we're going to cover here. Because the profit generally is not there as you're building up your audience to pay for slick marketing materials that a professional created. And, honestly, they're not needed for 99.9% of authors. Especially if you have a strong cover and use that in your ads. Because the cover is going to be doing most of the heavy lifting for you in terms of catching your audience's attention.

Also, mastering design basics will help you better judge the quality and appropriateness of any design work you do pay for, whether that's for your cover, your website, or your ads. Hopefully this book will also help you understand how easy or difficult something is to do. (For example, the first cover I ever paid for was an unmanipulated stock image that almost anyone could've put together in ten minutes, but I didn't know that at the time.)

Now, keep in mind when you're starting out with design work that you're probably going to make some mistakes or not have the skills to create the product you want. But just like with writing, you'll get better with practice, so don't give up on it.

As long as you're willing to try, fail, try again, fail again, try again, and succeed, you can get there. And I would bet good money that some of you who read this book will leave me in your dust in terms of where you end up.

The goal of this book is not to present myself as some untouchable expert but to instead share with you the foundational skills that I've learned.

Okay. So with that said, before we dive in on our first project I think it's important that we discuss some basic design principles that will help you create better images.

BASIC DESIGN PRINCIPLES

This is going to be a very high-level review of design principles. Ideally you should read more about it either online or by purchasing any of a number of books that are out there that cover these concepts. The two books on my shelf that are applicable to this are *The Non-Designer's Design Book* by Robin Williams and *Thou Shall Not Use Comic Sans* from Peachpit Press, but I'm sure there are others out there that also cover these concepts and are perhaps even better resources than those two.

I've also found a number of online articles and blogs that touch on these concepts, a few of which I'll mention below. This information is readily available for those who go looking.

Through all of this keep in mind that your goal is to (1) get the attention of *readers* who will like *your* type of book and then to (2) get them to click through and buy or download that book. Every design decision you make should revolve around those considerations.

With that said, let's start with color.

COLOR

There's actually a lot to think about with respect to color so remember that this is just a crash course.

GENRE-SPECIFIC

Most genres or categories use a specific color palette.

Many years ago and under a different pen name I published a few books about online dating. If you go and look at the books for men for online dating you'll see that for many of those books the colors that are used are white, black, red, and bright yellow.

In contrast, the colors that are used for books about online dating for women are white, black, and either pale or bright pink.

(I just double-checked and it looks like orange may be making its way in there as well for men, but even eight years later this still holds.)

This means that the very first thing you need to do before you choose your images or prepare an ad is look at books like yours and see what colors are in use in your genre or category.

This is probably more important when designing covers, but I think it is still important for ads. You can easily lose a reader if you don't use the colors that readers expect.

Say, for example, you're writing paranormal romance. If your colors are white, black, dark green, yellow, and gray that will confuse readers, because those colors don't really signify paranormal romance.

And I will add here that this is why it's good to read your genre because, especially on the Amazon storefront, books get so miscategorized that it can be tricky to do this research properly.

I just looked there to confirm my instinct that paranormal romance is usually a lot of bright purples and blues with some swirly movement involved. But there were books there by authors I wouldn't personally categorize as paranormal romance. Fantasy romance, yes. Paranormal, no.

So be careful and ideally look at authors who you know write what you write.

And if you don't know comparable authors, like I didn't for my romance titles, one place to look if you already have sales is at your also-boughts and also-reads on your book's product page. Although that can be biased by how you originally branded your title and the cover you chose, so it may not be perfect either, but it will at least get you closer to the target.

Also, you should know not only the colors for your genre, but the colors for your sub-genre, too. Romance is a huge genre, for example, and darker romance has a different color palette (dark background with white, red, bright yellow, maybe some lighter purple or turquoise text) than sweet and wholesome romance (white background with white, pink, light yellow, pale blue, lilac).

There are also color trends that can influence this, so make sure your research is current. I'd say color trends are more important on the non-fiction or literary fiction side than the genre fiction side, but they happen across all genres. Like the recent trend for a darker turquoise color on covers, and I believe it was a bright orange before that.

So. Genre and sub-genre appropriate and keep an eye on trends.

MEANING

The next thing to understand about colors, and this may be more for non-fiction than fiction or already baked into the genre-specific colors, is that colors have associated emotions and meanings.

I have a printout from some website called thelogocompany.net from 2013 that is a Color Emotion Guide. Looks like it's still available here: https://thelogocompany.net/psychology-of-color-in-logo-design/

It shows that colors like gray are for peace and calm whereas colors like red are for excitement or boldness. It also shows various brands that use those different colors. So, Fanta, for example is orange because it's a friendly, confident, and cheerful brand.

It's been a while since I did research on the meaning of color, but as I recall, not everyone agrees on the meaning behind every color.

Also, keep in mind that different colors have different meanings in different cultures. So one color may work great for the U.S. market but not for the Chinese market. I primarily sell in the U.S. so that's the market I design for, but if you're marketing say, a German translation, then it would be a good idea to know the meaning of different colors in Germany.

While there is likely no single definitive answer on color meaning you should at least have some idea about whether the ones you've chosen fit the book you're advertising.

A bright yellow color in an ad for a brutal, dark horror is going to attract the wrong reader because yellow is generally a happy, positive color.

(Unless it's clearly done in some sort of ironic way in which case that packaging better be spot on from ad through to book description. Because, again, the goal of ads and covers is to (a) attract someone to purchase your product, but to also (b) make sure it's the right person so they buy more from you later. Everything you do needs to be in alignment to pull in the *right* reader not just any reader. And that includes the colors you choose for your ads and covers.)

Now let's go into some more high-level color choice issues.

COLOR PAIRS

There is a reason so many movie posters use the colors orange and teal, and that's because orange and teal are considered complementary colors, they sit opposite one another on a color wheel.

A color wheel is created by taking the three primary colors, red, blue, and yellow and then combining them to get the secondary colors of purple, green, and orange. And then combining each secondary color with its neighboring primary colors to get tertiary colors such as yellow-orange, yellow-green, etc.

When in doubt about which colors to pair with one another, take the first color you want to use, like teal, and look directly across the color wheel to find the color that is opposite it, in this case, orange.

This is usually going to be an effective pairing.

Another option if you want a more subtle pairing is to stay with the same basic color but change the saturation or the brightness so that you pair a dark blue with a lighter shade of the same blue. This is essentially moving along a line drawn from the center of the color wheel to the outer edge.

(We'll see a color wheel later in Affinity. If you don't want to wait for that they're ubiquitous online, just search for color wheel.)

PRINT VERSUS SCREEN COLORS

Another issue you need to be aware of with respect to color is the difference between print color and screen color.

Ads and covers are designed on a computer screen, but the way that color is created on a computer screen is not the way that color is created when printed.

A screen uses what's called RGB colors which are created by combining different lights. RGB colors are brighter and more saturated and have a wider range of possibilities. Print uses CMYK colors which combine different inks.

For the ads we're going to be creating in this book, it's not going to be a big issue because we'll create on a screen and users will view on a screen. But do keep in mind that different displays will display colors differently. So, for example, I work on a PC but I also have a Mac and when I look at the same file on both computers, there is a clear difference between them. So know that your audience may see the image differently simply because they're viewing it on their hardware instead of yours.

CONTRAST

Another color issue to keep in mind when designing ads is that you want people to be able to see and absorb the key components of your ad.

This is why white on black and black on white are so common in signage because they contrast one another so strongly that you can see the text without struggle.

Some color combinations are horrible for contrast. I have seen the advice given, for example, to never put red on black or black on red. It's simply too hard to see. (I've broken this one before and currently have some covers that break this one, but it is true that it's harder to see.)

Whatever colors you choose, make sure that they contrast one another enough that your chosen elements are clearly visible to your audience.

(I say chosen elements because in some cases maybe we're not talking about text. For a fantasy my strongest ad element could be a dragon image. For a sexy romance ad it could be a hot guy. Whatever the element is that is supposed to draw in your reader, make sure it stands out. This is not the time for subtlety.)

Alright. That was the crash course in color, now on to element placement.

ELEMENT PLACEMENT

Element placement revolves around where you place each element of the design. This can be the book cover, review quote, ad image, promotional information, etc. There are tricks to make the placement of your elements more effective.

RULE OF THIRDS

One of the simplest ways to decide how to place the elements in your project is to use the rule of thirds. Take your document workspace and divide it into three horizontal sections and three vertical sections so that you end up with nine total sections.

If you can, you should then try to place pivotal elements at the intersection of these lines. The strongest intersection is the one in the top left corner.

You can also place the different elements of your design within the sections created by the grid to create a clean separation. Or line up a key portion of your image (such as the horizon or a tree or figure) along one of the lines.

This article by Cover Designs Studio (https://www.coverdesignstudio.com/layout-rule-of-thirds-diagonal-scan-and-more/) has a more detailed discussion of how this works and shows some real-life examples from trade-published book covers.

THE GOLDEN RATIO

Sometimes the rule of thirds can feel a little boring and basic. One of the ways I've experimented with mixing it up is trying to incorporate the golden ratio into my designs instead.

This basically involves using a rectangular space that has sides that are in the ratio of 1 to 1.618. You can then turn that on its side and create another, smaller rectangular space with the same ratio. Keep doing that and you end up with a series of smaller and smaller squares and a spiral down to a central point that will draw the eye.

Place a key element of your design in that central spot and it will be a more effective design.

I've tried using this with FB ads that use multiple images. I'm not sure I've been personally successful in those experiments. But the world abounds with examples of people who have successfully leveraged the golden ratio.

(Another possible way to use it is to use the 1.6 ratio when determining the relative font sizes of different text elements in your design.)

LEGIBILITY

The other key thing to keep in mind when creating an ad image is where and how your audience will view the image. In a FB feed, you don't want subtlety. This is not the time to have the outline of a dark gray dragon overlaid upon an even darker gray background.

If your ad doesn't convey something worth stopping for and clicking on, it's not an effective ad.

Now on to fonts.

FONT

Ah, font. So important and so easy to get wrong. This category covers the text choices you make—the actual font you use as well as its size and arrangement. It's much more important in cover design than in ad design, but we'll touch on a few key points at least.

TYPES AND HISTORY

Certain fonts are associated with key moments in history or have a bad reputation. (See Comic Sans for an example of a bad reputation.)

For example, if you find some cool font that you think will be just perfect for your project, maybe look it up first to make sure you aren't using the same font that was used for Word War II propaganda.

GENRE OR CATEGORY-SPECIFIC

Also, once more we run into the issue that certain genres or categories tend to use certain fonts or at least types of fonts. So, for example, a cursive font that looks like a woman's handwriting is more likely to be used for romance than for a thriller which is probably going to use a sans-serif font with some thickness to it instead.

If you're going to veer away from standard fonts for your ads, keep this in mind. Does the font match the genre or category of the book you're advertising? This is about conveying a consistent tone to your audience that tells them "this is the kind of book you want". If there's conflict between the font you use and the cover image, they probably won't click.

HIERARCHY

The important elements in your ad should be the largest elements in your ad. You don't want your audience's eye drawn to the wrong part of the ad first. Using a larger font size is one way to draw attention to key elements.

LEGIBILITY

Font can convey tone and genre outside of the words that are written, but if you're also trying to highlight a good quote, for example, you'll want your audience to be able to read the text of that quote. Always check that your ad will be legible at the size it will be seen by your audience which is often going to be much smaller than the size you design at.

* * *

Alright. That was your crash course in design elements. It's not everything, but it should be enough to get us started.

And if you want to dive in further on these topics there are many, many resources out there. The internet has any number of websites about design and there are a handful of free courses through Coursera and other sites.

Although I will say that I personally find the ones geared toward graphic design in general a bit annoying. I like to get to the point and those courses sometimes want to show me how to make artistic designs using an apple as a stamp or will spend an hour discussing the history of fonts. Zzzz.

Anyway. We're ready for our first project now, but first I want to talk about how to set up your workspace in Affinity when working with images like ads or covers.

AFFINITY WORKSPACE

I have Affinity Publisher set up very differently when I'm working with covers or ad creatives compared to when I'm laying out a book. By using Studio Presets I can switch back and forth between the two without having to reconfigure my workspace each time.

I already covered this in *Affinity Publisher for Fiction Layouts* from the print layout perspective, so if you've read that book and already created a workspace for images, then you can skim this section. But I expect that there will be enough readers who wanted to learn ad creatives but not book layouts that I better cover it again here to be safe.

(I am going to skip over the "what is Affinity" and how to open it portion, though.)

Okay. So setting up your workspace.

First I'm going to show you my workspace with a simple project already open so you can see the various components you'll be working with as you do your design work.

Here we go:

This is a simple image I put together in Affinity Publisher for the video course *Affinity Publisher Quick Takes.*

In the center is the image I created.

On the left-hand side of the workspace you can see a number of small icons like the ones in the screenshot below which each correspond to a different tool available to you in Publisher:

These icons will always be there by default when you have a project open and we are going to use them a lot throughout this book.

When I work on image-heavy projects like ads or covers that is all I have on the left-hand side. (For print layouts I put a number of my often-used studios over there, but not for image-heavy projects. I want as much of my screen space for my design as I can get.)

Along the top of the workspace are options that will change depending upon the tool you have selected on the left-hand side. I may sometimes refer to this as the dynamic toolbar.

Here are a few that are visible when I have the Artistic Text Tool (the capital A) selected.

There are dropdowns there for font, font style, and font size as well as options to click on for bolded, italicized, and underlined text.

A lot of the text-based work and image alignment we do will be done using these top options.

The bold and italic options will only be available if the font you choose has those versions. Unlike when working in Microsoft Word not all fonts you choose will have a bold or italic option. On the other hand, some fonts will have multiple "bold" weights to choose from. In general in Affinity I use the dropdown that says "Regular" to see the available weights for the font I'm using rather than clicking on the B for bold.

Okay. Moving on.

On the right-hand side of the workspace are where I place what Affinity calls studios. I think of them as task panes devoted to specific topics and there are a number of them that I like to keep open for quick use.

Studios can be opened or closed using the View option in the top menu. Go to View->Studio to see your list of available studios.

Those that are already open will show with a checkmark next to the name. Here you can see, for example, that the Character, Color, and Glyph Browser studios are already open but the Anchor, Assets, Constraints, and other listed studios are not.

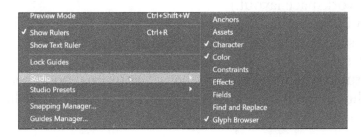

To add a studio to the workspace, click on its name in the dropdown menu. A studio that you open is going to open on top of your workspace in a separate dialogue box. You can left-click and drag on that dialogue box to dock it to the left or right side of the workspace.

By default Affinity has studios docked on the top-left as well as the top, middle, and bottom right. As you can see, for design work I dock most of my studios in the top right corner and then move between them by clicking on the tabs at the top of the section.

When a dialogue box is in a position where it can be docked, you should see a light blue highlight. You can then release the left-click and it should stay in that position. When you drag a newly-opened studio dialogue box to a position where there already is one, it will look like a file tab at the top. Drag to the left or right to position the studio in your desired order relative to the other studios that are already there.

If you have a studio docked that you don't want, you can left-click on it, drag it away from where it's docked, and then click on the X in the top right corner to close it. Or you can go to View->Studio and click on its name in the secondary dropdown menu to uncheck it.

So which studios do I keep open? Let's zoom in on the top section of my workspace to see:

In the image above the Layers studio is currently open, but you can also see the abbreviations for the Pages, Character, Glyph Browser, Text Frame, Swatches, and Color studios. Pages is to the left, the rest are to the right.

I'm going to walk through each one and as I do I recommend that you open and dock it in the same order that I have them so that my screenshots match your workspace. (You don't have to, it'll just make it easier to use this book if we both have the same workspace layout.)

The first tab I have is the Pages studio. By default I believe it is docked on the left-hand side, so left-click on its name and drag to the right-hand side if you want your workspace to look like mine.

The Pages studio will give you a preview of your final document. For example, here is what the image in the workspace would actually look like if I were to export it right now:

Note that the blue line around the text that's visible in the main workspace is gone and also that the image no longer extends past the edge of the rectangle.

(That gray line around the perimeter is not, however, part of the final image. That's just how it looks when in the Pages studio.)

For design work, I don't use this one all that often, but it's still nice to have pinned to my workspace.

The next studio I have in that top section is the Layers studio.

By default I believe it's docked in the middle on the right-hand side, so you'd need to click and drag it up to have the same layout that I use. (I don't like to have any studios in the middle because when you have a lot of layers having those studios there cuts off how many layers you can see at one time.)

The Layers studio is the primary studio I use for design work. This is where you can move items around to make sure that, for example, your text is on top of your image not behind it.

It is also where you can select the correct component to work on. And it's where you can group layers so that they can be moved around together or adjusted together.

Finally, it's where you can turn on or off some image effects and hide or unhide layers. All things that you may want to do as you design your ads.

We will spend a lot more time with this one don't worry.

After that, I have the Character studio.

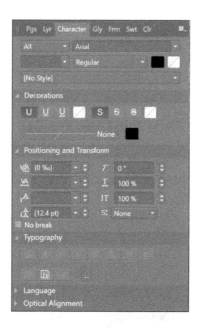

I believe it too is by default in the center on the right-hand side.

This is another one I don't use a lot but it's nice to have handy when I need it. Most of the basic text formatting options are available at the top of the workspace, so you shouldn't need to come here to change the font or font style, although you can.

What it can be useful for is adjusting the kerning or tracking of your text or using all caps or subscripts or superscripts. Basically, more fancy manipulations of your text are found here.

Next I have the Glyph Browser studio.

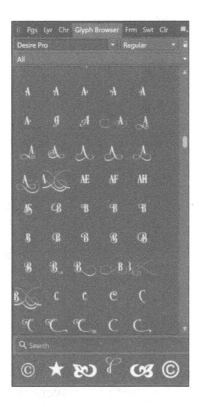

This is not one I believe is open by default so if you want it you'll need to open it via the View menu up top and then dock it. This one is good for when you need to insert design elements that are part of a font or for any font you use that has a lot of variants.

If you look in the main space of the screenshot above you can see that with the Desire Pro font I have seventeen different versions of the capital letter A to choose from, some very basic, some incredibly ornate. (And actually if I scroll up there are ten more choices for the capital letter A, so I have twenty-seven total choices.)

Rather than remember keyboard shortcuts to get each variation, I can just go to the glyph browser studio and double-click on the one I want to use.

In the section below that, you can also see my recently used glyphs for an idea of what else I pull into my designs using the glyph browser.

That star shape is available under the main Wingdings font and is perfect for use in ads where you want to include five stars before the text of a review. This is also how I pull in decorative elements for breaks between text in my ads.

After the glyph browser I have the Text Frame studio.

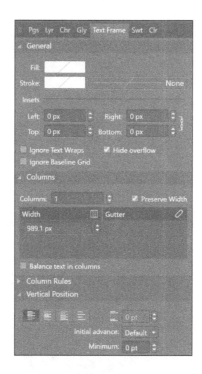

This is another one I don't believe is available by default but that I like to use often enough that I pull it in. It's more for covers than ads, though.

I often use text frames because putting text in a text frame is a good way to have that text aligned within just that frame instead of the entire space you're working in.

After that I have the Swatches studio.

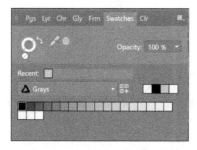

That one is in the top right section by default I believe, so it's just a matter of moving it one to the left past the Color studio. (Left-click, drag, release when in position.)

The Swatches studio is the easiest way to change a color element to black or white. Just click on the swatch square for that color after you've selected whatever it is you need to change.

You can also see there that it shows your current filler color (the filled-in circle) and current outline color (the doughnut shape) at the top. Whichever one of those two is displaying on top is the one that's currently available to use. Click on the other to bring it to the forefront.

A white circle with a red line through it means no color.

You can always change one or the other back to no color using the small white circle with a line through it at the bottom left corner of the two options.

The Swatches studio also allows you to use the eyedropper to select a color from your image. You do have to then double-click on that color to apply it as either the fill color or border color, whichever is currently selected.

Also, once you're working with your document and have used various colors, the Recent section will show square swatches for all colors you've used in the document. This makes it easy to use the same color on multiple components.

The final studio I have in the top right section is the Color studio, which is located there by default. This is the studio that lets you really get wild with colors.

In the default view, you can click on that colored rainbow to choose a general color and then click below to choose any of a range of variations on that color. Or you can change the dropdown to Saturation or Lightness to see the colors presented in a different layout.

You can also adjust the opacity of a color. The lower the opacity the more you can see what's behind it.

This is also where I will double-click on the circle with my current color to bring up the color chooser if I have specific color values I want to use.

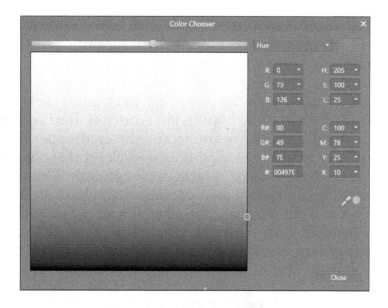

For example, I've found a bright yellow that I like to use for covers and advertisements that displays well and isn't too green or too pale, so I always just input its values using the color chooser when I need to use it.

The Color Chooser is also where you can find the color wheel we discussed earlier.

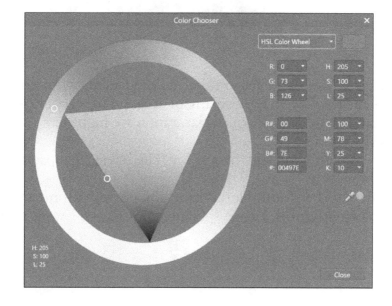

Remember how I said you can draw a line across the circle to find a complementary color to the one you're using? This is where you would do so visually. Just mentally draw a line across from your current color and then click.

Affinity also has studios available in the default view that I don't use. It looks like they start with the Stroke studio in the top right and the Paragraph and Text Styles studios in the middle right.

If you don't want them there, you can left-click and drag each one out to the middle of your workspace and then click on the X in the top right corner to close them. Same for the Assets and Stock studios on the left-hand side.

That leaves us with the bottom right-hand section. The only studio I keep down there is the Transform studio.

This one is very important. It's where you can see the relative position of an object within the workspace and also the overall dimensions of that object. I will often go to this studio to adjust the size of an image proportionately.

Affinity appears to also by default have the History and Navigator studios here. I rarely if ever use either one. You can leave them there if you want or remove them. Up to you. We won't use them here but you may see them in some of my screenshots just because I didn't remove them before I took my screenshots.

Okay, so that's my set-up. As you learn Affinity you will find the layout that works best for you.

Once you arrange your studios to your liking, I recommend that you save that set-up as a Preset.

To do so, go to View->Studio Presets->Add Preset and type in a name for your preset and then click OK.

Once you've done that, you can always go back to that layout by going to View->Studio Presets and then clicking on the name for your preset under the secondary dropdown menu. So don't be afraid to move things around and experiment a bit. As long as you've saved your layout as a preset, it's always going to be there to go back to.

Let's say you have a preset and then you change your layout and like it better. To save over that existing preset, just act as if you're creating a new preset by choosing Add Preset and give it the exact same name as your old preset. That will overwrite the old layout with your new one.

I love presets, because they let me move back and forth between the very different sets of tools that I use for print interior layouts and ad and cover design.

Finally, to go back to Affinity's default arrangement, I believe you can use View->Studio->Reset Studio. (That's the layout I was talking from when I said that I think that Affinity is by default laid out X way, but I've been working with my presets so long I don't want to swear to it.)

Alright then. Now that we have our workspace arranged, it's time for our first project, which is to take an existing ebook cover image and create an image to upload for use in an Amazon A+ Content Standard Comparison Chart module.

COVER IMAGE FOR USE IN AN AMAZON A+ COMPARISON CHART

One of the issues I've run into on Amazon is that they list my large print books in the same section as the regular-sized print books, which means that someone has to be fairly savvy to find the large print edition of a book. Since with my cozies I assume those are my older readers, I don't want them to have to go through that kind of effort to find the next book in the series.

To get around this issue I leverage Amazon's A+ Content Standard Comparison Chart module. It allows me to provide an image of each book cover, a link to that book, and then random information that I provide to justify the use of the comparison chart module.

Here is an example:

Each of the titles there is a hyperlink to that edition of the book. I list the various formats just because I have to list at least one piece of information in order to use the comparison chart.

Easy enough to do and it solves my problem.

But the image specifications that Amazon lists are not in line with standard cover dimensions. If you go into the A+ Content Manager and you click on Standard Comparison Chart for your module, you'll see this:

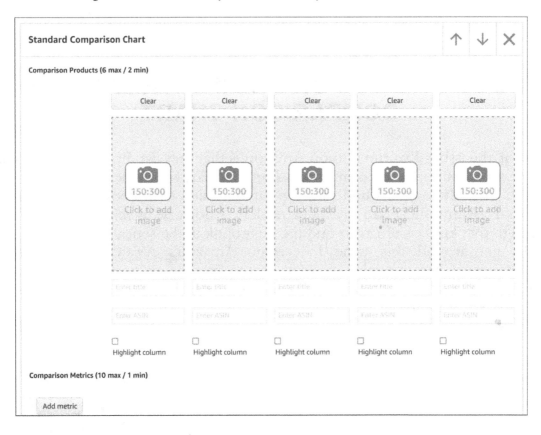

Note that the image it wants you to upload is 150:300. That's a 1:2 ratio whereas most covers are a 1:1.6 ratio. Which means that you can't just try to upload your cover, you have to create a modified JPG file for upload.

Let's do that now. It's good practice for working with images in Affinity Publisher.

First things first, open Affinity Publisher, close out any notices about new versions, and then click on New Document in the dialogue box or go to File->New if you've already closed that out.

This will bring up the New Document dialogue box. Click on the web option at the top and then click on one of the listed layouts below that.

On the right-hand side, make sure the page orientation is set to portrait and change the Page Width and Page Height values to 150 and 300 respectively. Here's an example where I've done that with arrows pointing to the respective values:

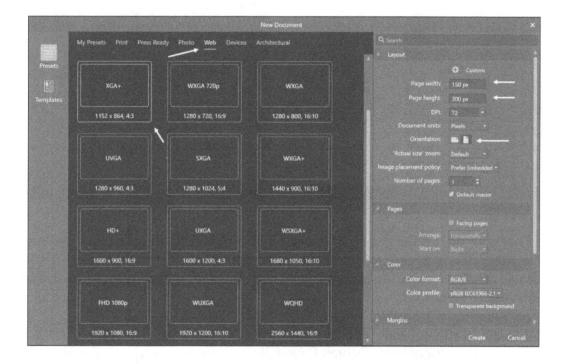

A DPI of 72 and RGB/8 for the color format should be fine.

You can up the DPI if you want. I have mine set to 96 for some reason and some of the templates in the web section use 144. For what we're doing here as long as your setting is at least 72, it should work.

(I'm not going to have you create a preset for this one, because it's better for you to work from the final file we're going to create when you need additional images. That will ensure that all of your images are the exact same size. If you don't know what I'm talking about right now, don't worry, we'll cover it later.)

Okay. Once you've changed those settings, click Create.

You should end up with a workspace that looks something like this:

The Layers studio on the right has just one layer, Master A, and the main workspace shows the blank canvas we asked Affinity to create that's 150 by 300 pixels. You can see those dimensions by looking at the W and H values in the Transform studio in the bottom right corner.

Very exciting. (Or not.)

I'm now going to walk you through two separate ways to place the cover image into your document. (Note: This will work for any image you want to use, not just your cover.)

But first, before we go any further, make sure that you have snapping enabled. It's under the dropdown at the top of the screen that has a horseshoe-shaped magnet. Click on that icon and make sure that the Enable Snapping checkbox is checked.

Once snapping is enabled, Affinity will show you red and green lines when you drag your elements around and they align with either other elements in your layout or with the edges of your canvas.

Using these lines is the easiest way to draw out a frame or image to the proper size and to move it around within your workspace and ensure it's aligned or centered.

Okay. Let's place your cover image now.

Option one is to place your cover directly onto the workspace. To do that, go to the left-hand side of the workspace and click on the icon that looks like a painting of a landscape. If you hold your mouse over it, you will see that it is called the Place Image Tool.

Clicking on that icon will bring up an Open dialogue box. Navigate to where you have your cover saved and select it. Once you've done that, click on Open at the bottom of the dialogue box.

Next you want to left-click on the edge of your workspace about a little over midway up on the left-hand side. Hold that left-click as you drag down and to the right. As you do so, the cover should appear in the white space and increase in size.

Drag all the way to the bottom of the white space. You should see a red line appear across the bottom of the white space when the bottom of the cover aligns to the bottom of the white space.

If you go too far, just move back up until you see that red line. Release the left-click.

When you're done, unless you're a genius at judging dimensions, you should have a cover image that is aligned along the left-hand side of the white space and along the bottom of the white space, but is not yet aligned to the right of the white space. Like so:

To fix this, click on the blue circle in the top right corner of the cover image and drag at an angle until the cover entirely fills the white space.

When you hit the edge of the white space on the right-hand side you should see a green line appear. Release your left-click.

You should end up with something like this that has your cover at the bottom and filling the space completely from left to right but with white space remaining above:

It should not go past the edges of your canvas.

And that's it. You're done. All you need to do is export as a JPG image and save the file so you can use it again.

Options two is to use a Picture Frame first and then drop the cover into the picture frame.

By using a picture frame and then swapping out your image (which we'll cover in a moment) you can ensure that your A+ Content images will always be the same size.

If you're writing fiction and using standard print and ebook dimensions, you probably won't need to do that. You can just use the ebook cover and click and drag on each edge until you see the green and red lines along the edges like we just discussed. That should result in same-sized images each time as long as your ebook covers are all the same dimension and you line them up along the left, bottom, and right sides.

But I do use a picture frame. For two reasons.

First, because most of my non-fiction books are not in standard ebook dimensions and I want to display the print covers in my A+ content not the ebook covers.

The easiest way to do so is by using the PDF I create for the print cover. But that requires sizing the image so that the small excess along the edges of the print template is trimmed away.

Because that's not an exact adjustment, if I did it freehand I'd end up with slightly different image sizes each time. (Ask me how I know...)

The other reason is because some of my older ebook covers were created at a different dimension than my newer ones. Using a picture frame ensures that I'm always going to be creating an image for my A+ content that is the same size.

Okay. That was a lot of talking that probably sounded confusing. Let's go do an example and you'll see what I mean.

If you don't have a print template of your cover, just follow along here and keep it in mind for later.

First, we need to go back to the plain white canvas from before.

If you were following along with me in the first step and so currently have a copy of your cover in your workspace, go to the Layers studio, right-click on the layer that contains the image of your cover, and choose Delete from the dropdown menu.

That will remove that layer and take you back to the blank canvas we had before. Alternatively, you can also use Ctrl + Z to Undo back to before the point where you inserted your cover image. Either way, you should be back to a blank canvas before the next step.

Now go back to the left-hand set of icons we used before but this time click on the Picture Frame Rectangle Tool. It's the rectangular image with an X across it that's, at least for me, the eighth one down if you start counting from the black arrow for the Move Tool option.

Once you've selected the picture frame tool, left-click and drag from the edge of the white space like you did before when you were inserting your cover. This time when you do so it will form a rectangle with an X in it.

You want the shape you create to be aligned along the left, bottom, and right of the white space and to be the approximate shape of a book cover. If it isn't, you can click on the blue circles along the perimeter of the rectangle and drag each line until it is aligned with the edge and your image is the correct proportions or thereabouts.

When I do this for a 7.5 x 9.25 inch print cover, I end up with something like this:

Now it's time to place an image in that frame.

To do so, click on the Place Image Tool that we used before (that looks like a landscape drawing), navigate to the image you want to use, and select it.

Affinity should automatically insert the image into your picture frame as long as you didn't click away from the picture frame in the interim.

Here I've place a PDF of the paperback cover that was the KDP cover version for one of my non-fiction titles.

I prefer to use the KDP version because it's just the cover, there's no extra white space around it like with IngramSpark covers, but either one will work just fine because all that will show in the final image is what's inside the frame, as you can see above.

I inserted the full cover, but you can see that it's cut off. It actually extends to the right and left, but because we're using a picture frame those portions of the image outside of the frame are not visible to us.

If I'd placed the image directly without using that frame the whole image would show in my workspace (we'll see an example of that later), but still would not show in my final exported image. In a situation like that, you can see what would export by going to the Pages studio. I personally find that hard to work with, so I tend to use picture frames a lot.

Like we're doing here. So we have the picture frame and we have the image that's been inserted into it, but we're seeing the wrong part of the image right now.

The next step is to move the image we inserted so that we're seeing the front cover in the frame.

There are two ways to do this. One is to left-click and drag from the center of the four arrows that should be visible in the center of the image.

The other is to go to the image layer first in the Layers studio, like here:

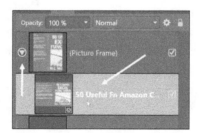

And then click and drag the image like any other object. Use the Move Tool to be able to click anywhere on the image. Otherwise click from the perimeter.

This is what I get initially when I move my cover around:

You can see the blue border that represents the border of the image I'm working with, but note how only the portion of the image that's in the picture frame is visible in the workspace.

Now, I was guesstimating the size of the picture frame when I inserted it and you likely will be too. And chances are you won't get it right the first time around.

For example, here I'm seeing too much of the colored background on the top and bottom. I'd prefer it was about the same amount as we're seeing on the left and right sides. Which means I need to adjust the picture frame so that it's a little shorter.

To do so, I can go to the Layers studio and click on the layer for the picture frame. (Remember that we're currently clicked onto the image that's indented below that.)

Clicking on the picture frame ensures that any edits are going to be made to the picture frame, not the image it contains.

Once you've done that, go back to the workspace, click on the blue circles along the edge of the frame and drag them to adjust the frame to the size you want.

In my case, I click on the blue circle at the top and drag downward to make my text frame shorter.

Since I know I'm going to need to reposition my image to center it again in my resized picture frame, I bring the edge of the picture frame almost down to the top line of text in the cover:

Once my picture frame is resized, I can once more click and drag to center the cover in the newly-resized picture frame.

Sometimes you'll have to move back and forth between the frame and the image a few times to get it right. You may even need to resize the image at some point.

(To resize the image you can usually use the slider below the image. Either that or select the image layer in the Layers studio and then click and drag the image from the corner or change its size in the Transform studio with Lock Aspect Ratio on.)

Also, remember that Ctrl + Z, Undo, does work in Affinity Publisher.

So if you accidentally adjust the picture frame instead of the picture or the picture instead of the picture frame, just use Ctrl + Z to undo and then go back and click on the appropriate layer in the Layers studio before you try again.

(This can come in handy, too, when Affinity decides to change both the picture frame and the underlying image at the same time. Usually that happens if you don't have the picture frame layer expanded in the Layers studio at the time you try to change its size.)

Anyway. Ultimately after I made my adjustments I ended up with this:

That works.

It's a subtle difference, but you can see that the portion of the cover on the top and bottom that is a solid color is now smaller and more in proportion to the sides. This now looks more like the actual print cover does when the book is printed.

Whichever of the above methods you use, once you're done you're going to want to export the image as a JPG file. (See the later chapter for how to export images.) You can then upload it to Amazon and it will look like this:

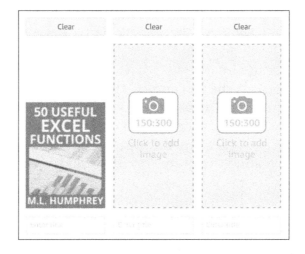

Note how the white space above the cover simply disappears and it looks like you just uploaded your cover and nothing else.

Perfect.

Also, for this one, save the final file for future use. (File->Save)

The reason you want to save a copy of the file and use it again is because once you've set up your first comparison content file, it's very, very easy to swap in a new cover without having to redo all the work we just did.

And it's better to swap out the covers if they're the same dimensions because that will ensure that the A+ content image dimensions are exactly the same each time.

Let me show you how to do that now.

With your final file open, go to Document->Resource Manager. This will bring up the Resource Manager dialogue box which will show you all of the images that are in your document.

In this case, we just have the one.

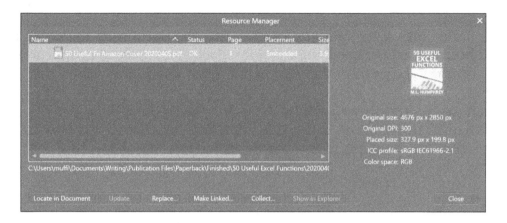

Click on that listing for the image like I have above—it will highlight in blue—and then click on Replace at the bottom of the dialogue box.

In the Open dialogue box that appears, navigate to where the next cover image you want to use is saved, select it, and choose Open.

Your other option is to click on the image layer and then use the Replace Image option in the dynamic menu up top. It should be visible when the Move Tool or Picture Frame Tool is selected.

Either option will bring in that replacement image in the exact same location as the one that you used previously. For ebook covers, that should be all you have to do. They're generally going to be the exact same dimensions so there's no adjustment to be made.

For print covers, you will likely need to move the cover image right or left because the different spine widths for print books make the files different sizes which means Affinity will place them differently.

If you do need to make an adjustment when working with a picture frame, be sure to make it to the *image* layer not the *picture frame* layer. The picture frame layer is what keeps everything looking uniform and the same size. If you change the picture frame then your images will not match up when they're side-by-side.

Also, assuming the two images were created the same way, try to limit your adjustments to moving the image left or right. If you resize the new image, it may look wrong when set next to the old image because, for example, the text will be bigger or smaller between the two images.

If you do find yourself having to resize your second image, then you may want to consider going back and redoing your first one so that they match in terms of overall size and relative size.

This is, of course, assuming the source files were the same general dimensions.

(It won't normally be that big of an issue and you're probably going to be dealing with ebook covers so it shouldn't be any issue at all, but it might happen so I wanted to cover it just in case.)

Okay. Done. That was how to create the 150:300 image you need for an Amazon A+ Content Comparison Chart. Now on to something more custom. Let's talk about how to create an image that shows all of your book covers for use on an A+ Content page, FB banner, or website banner.

BANNER IMAGE CONTAINING MULTIPLE BOOK COVERS

The example we're going to do here is for A+ Content, but honestly, change the dimensions up and it could be for a Facebook banner or a webpage banner or any of a number of other advertising options.

What we're going to create is something that looks like this:

This is probably far more complex than most authors will need, but doing one with this many covers allows me to show you a few extra tricks you can use in Affinity. And the skills we're going to cover here will work as well for three covers as they do for ten.

* * *

First things first, where can you get the three-dimensional images for your covers?

If you're really lucky your cover designer provided you with one. And, even better, it was a PNG file with a transparent background.

I have one that my cover designer provided that was a JPG file with a white background that makes it very challenging to use in a lot of settings. So if, like me and many others, you are not lucky enough to have a usable file from your cover designer, you have a couple of other options.

Option two is to use Book Brush (https://bookbrush.com) to create a three-dimensional cover. Last I checked they offered fifteen free downloads, so you could easily get enough of your covers done that way to create what we're going to do here for free. And they're also reasonably priced if you have more covers than that.

Option three is to use Affinity *Photo*. If you have Affinity Photo then you can go to Covervault (https://covervault.com) and download one of their free book mockups. For this example I used the 5.5 x 8.5 Standing Paperback Book Mockup.

In Affinity Photo change your Preferences so that "Import PSD smart objects where possible" is checked. This will allow you to open most mockup templates which are usually created as PSD files for Photoshop.

Once you open the mockup file in Affinity Photo it's just a matter of double-clicking on the embedded document layer for the cover where you can then insert the cover image using File->Place which is very much like using the Place Image Tool in Publisher.

If the image doesn't fit the space perfectly, you may also need to use the Flood Fill Tool on the left-hand side (looks like a paint bucket) to fill in the background with your cover color. Or you'll need to stretch the cover a bit to fit the space.

From here on out, I'm going to assume that you've used one of the above options and that you have three-dimensional versions of your covers to work with. If you don't, you can do this with two-dimensional covers instead.

* * *

For this project, we're going to once more use picture frames and work with replacing images, but we're also going to learn how to select multiple layers, group layers, duplicate layers, align objects, and add a colored background in Publisher.

Okay. First things first, we need a new document to work in. The A+ Content module I use for this is 970 pixels by 600 pixels.

So go to File->New, choose one of the Web presets, and modify the pixel size to 970 by 600. 72 DPI is fine. It should be landscape. And RGB/8 is fine for the color. This will give you a big white rectangle in your workspace.

Next we need to add a colored background.

To do this, you want the Rectangle Tool which is the blue-colored square icon about seven down on the left-hand side of the workspace. We're just going to click on the blue square, but if you click on the little white arrow in the bottom right corner you can see all sorts of other shapes that are available in Affinity.

Click on the Rectangle Tool, then left-click in a corner of the white canvas in your workspace and hold that left-click down as you drag at a diagonal to the opposite corner. Your goal is to cover the entire canvas with this rectangle. You should see the green and red snapping lines when you hit the edge of the canvas.

If you let up on the left-click without reaching the edges or go too far, you can left-click on the blue circles around the perimeter and drag each edge into alignment separately.

Depending on what color you had as your Fill color it may not look like you changed much. Mine is a light gray so it really isn't noticeable. But if you look in the Layers studio you will now see that you have a Rectangle layer in addition to your Master layer.

Let's go ahead and make our rectangle black instead.

Above the workspace in the dynamic menu area, you should see a Fill option with a small rounded rectangle next to it that shows the same color as the rectangle you just drew. Click on that rounded rectangle to open a dropdown dialogue box with color options.

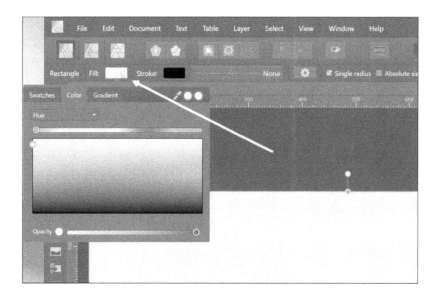

Mine opened to the Color tab, but since I just want a black background, I am going to click on the Swatches tab, and then the square swatch for black. That will turn my rectangle in my workspace into a solid black rectangle instead of light gray like it was before.

The Swatches tab is the best option for black, grays, or white. The Color tab is better for actual colors as you can see with the rainbow of options and then the various iterations of those colors that show below in the screenshot above.

Click on the rainbow to select the color you want and then click anywhere in that large rectangular space to select the specific shade of the color.

Now that our background is in place we're ready to add our cover images.

I like to do this with picture frames so that everything is the same size and I don't have to worry about the perimeter of two images overlapping. This is especially true with 3D covers which often come with extraneous space around the actual cover. By using a picture frame, only the cover portion of the image that I place in the frame will show in my design.

Okay. So we need to start with a picture frame. Click on the Picture Frame Rectangle Tool we used before and then left-click and draw a shape on the canvas in your workspace that's about 200 pixels tall by 125 pixels wide.

You should be able to see the dimensions as you click and drag to form your shape. Mine came out to a W of 128.8 and an H of 197.3.

If you want exact measurements, go down to the Transform studio and type those values into your W and H fields like here where I've changed them to 125 and 200:

Next, click on the Place Image Tool and go find your first 3D cover.

If you haven't clicked away from the picture frame, it should insert the image directly into your frame, like so:

Adjust the position of your cover so that it's centered in the box you created and so that it also fills most of the space.

Remember, you can either use the slider below the image to change its size and click in the center of the four arrows in the center of the image to click and drag to reposition the image, or you can go to the Layers studio and click down to the image layer before trying to move or resize the image like any other element.

If you use the image layer option, you should place a border around the image first (which we're going to do next) so that you can see the borders of the picture frame as you reposition the image.

I'm going to place a border because that's what Affinity will use for alignment with other elements. First, though, I want to hide the black background layer.

I can do that by going to the Layers studio and unchecking the box for that layer.

Once I'm working on a white background, I can then click on the picture frame layer in the Layers studio and in the dynamic menu above the workspace click on the white line with a red slash through it next to Stroke to add a line around the frame by moving the slider for Width to the right until there is a visible frame around my image. Like so:

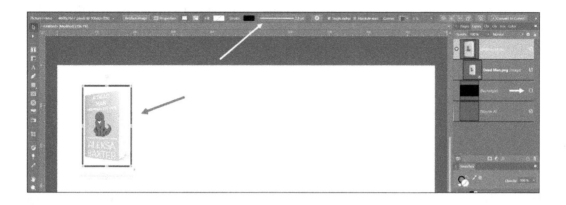

You can see that the width of the line around the frame is now 3.8.

That lets me see the borders of my frame at all times.

After I manually increase the size of the image a bit and also move it around until it is centered top to bottom and side to side, here's what I ultimately end up with:

I had to center the image manually because the underlying image does not have the book cover centered. This is an issue you will probably run into with most of the 3D cover templates that are available for free.

The nice thing about using a black border for the picture frame when I have a black background is it's going to blend right in when I turn the background layer back on so I don't have to remove it. In the meantime it will let me see the boundaries Affinity is using for aligning my cover images to one another.

Fortunately, we only needed to do all of that positioning once, because we can just swap in all of the other covers for this one at the end since they're all the exact same size. Which means our next step is to copy the picture frame and cover we just created nine more times.

One fun trick that Affinity does when you copy an object is that if you copy the object and then move it and then make another copy, Affinity will paste *and move* that second copy. Which means that you only have to move the first copy you make, Affinity will space out the other copies for you.

It's maybe best understood in action.

Below what I did is clicked onto the Picture Frame layer in the Layers studio, right-clicked, and chose Duplicate. I then clicked onto the picture frame in my workspace and dragged the duplicated image over so that I had two duplicate images side by side like so:

After that I could just right-click and Duplicate that layer in the Layers studio three more times and what I ended up with was five covers in picture frames, all evenly spaced.

Basically, Affinity saved me a little bit of clicking and dragging for each image I copied.

So that's the first five covers. Rather than repeat that five more times, we can now group those covers and copy the group.

To do so, go to the Layers studio, click on the top or bottommost of the picture frame layers, hold down the shift key, and click on the other end of the range of picture frame layers.

You should see all five of the layers highlighted in blue like this:

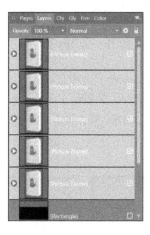

Use Ctrl + G to group them. You could also right-click and choose Group from the dropdown menu, but Ctrl + G is faster and you'll use it often enough it's worth memorizing.

When you group the picture frames, this will create a primary layer called Group in your Layers studio.

You can still click on the arrow next to the Group layer name to expand the group and see each of the individual picture frame layers below it.

If you want to rename the group, you can click on the name (Group) and then type in a new name. For complex projects it probably makes sense to do so. For something like this I don't bother.

The nice thing about grouping objects is you can then move them around together as one item.

You can also resize the entire group together. For example, maybe I want covers that are 250 pixels tall now that I'm looking at this. That would fill out my background better.

Rather than change the height of every one of the five picture frames, I can click onto the group layer in my Layers studio and then go to my canvas and click on the blue circle in any corner and drag at an angle to resize the entire group at once.

(I could click on that Group layer in the Layers studio and change the dimensions in the Transform studio, but I'd need to remember to Lock Aspect Ratio before I did that or my images would skew.)

Here's what I get in my workspace when I select the group and click and drag to resize all of the covers at once:

But I still have an issue, which is that the covers are evenly spaced compared to one another but they are not evenly spaced across my canvas. Right now the covers are more to the right side of the canvas than the left.

Also, they need to be spaced apart from one another a little bit more because even centered I'm going to have too much space along the outer edges.

First things first, let's center the group as it exists right now.

To do so, make sure you're clicked on the group layer in the Layers studio and then go to the Alignment option at the top of the workspace, which is a bar with two blue lines coming off the right-hand side. Clicking on that will open the alignment dropdown menu. Under Align Horizontally click on the Align Center option:

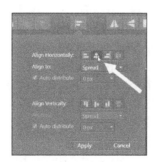

When you do this Affinity will center the entire group on your canvas based upon where the outer edge of the first cover is and where the outer edge of the last cover is.

(This is why using picture frames helps so much because an uneven image may have 25 pixels on the left and 100 on the right so that even though it looks fine on the canvas because that difference blends into the background it won't look right if you try to center it.)

Okay. Anyway. This is what I get when I center my group of five covers:

You can see that the amount of white space on the left of the first cover is more than the amount of white space between each of the covers. Which may actually be fine. We're going to end up with some space on the top and bottom and that may actually match up with the space there and look fine.

But let's say I want the covers to be closer to the edge, which means I need to spread them out more. Affinity will space them evenly for me, but I first need to move the covers on the left and right out to where I want the outer edge to be on each side.

To do so, I go to the Layers studio, expand the Group layer, click on the picture frame layer for the left-most cover image, and then go back into the workspace and move that frame to the left until it's where I want it to be. I then do the same for the right-most cover.

(You could technically just move one of the covers, but I prefer to move both because it lets me better establish my outer edges. If I only did one I'd have to mentally adjust where I placed it based upon the fact that I'd be re-centering my group when I was done.)

Okay. So doing that will give you something like this:

See how there's more space between the first and second frames now? And between the fourth and fifth? But how my first and last covers are closer to the outer edge and have about the same amount of space between their outer edge and edge of my canvas?

Now I need Affinity to evenly space my picture frames across this amount of expanded space.

My first step is to go into the Layers studio and select the layers for all five covers (click on the bottommost one, Shift, click on the topmost one). Next, I go up to the Alignment option once more but this time I choose the Space Vertically option under Align Horizontally. It's the one on the far right.

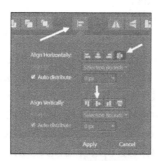

While we're there we can also click on Align Middle under the Align Vertically section just in case when I dragged one of the covers over I also dragged it up or down a little bit.

What that gives me is all five covers spaced out equally between the outer edge of the picture frame for the first cover and the outer edge of the picture frame for the last cover with all of the frames also aligned along the top and bottom edge as well.

Perfect.

Now that we have our first row of covers set up the way we want them, we just need to duplicate this group to create our second row of covers.

To do so, I go back to the Group layer in the Layers studio, right-click, and choose Duplicate from the dropdown menu. I can then click on the visible covers in the canvas and drag down the duplicated layer so it doesn't overlap the original one.

I could try to manually center and space the two rows, but it's easier to let Affinity do it for me. To do that, select both groups in the Layers studio (using the Ctrl key if they're not next to one another) and then go to the Alignment option at the top of the workspace.

This time we want to Align Center under Align Horizontally but we need to use Spread as the parameter. And then under Align Vertical we can click on Space Vertically and use the auto distribute setting to spread the two rows apart from one another. I chose 32 pixels as a good distance between the two rows.

Next, create a new group from the two row groups in the Layers studio. Go back to the Alignment option and this time choose Align Middle under Align Vertically. That will center the combination of the two rows top to bottom so that they have an equal amount of space above and below the two rows

Turn back on the background layer by checking its box in the Layers studio and you should have something that looks like this:

(The apparent downward versus upward angle of the covers in the two rows is just an optical illusion, because all ten images are the exact same image.)

Okay. All that's left to do is to swap out the covers. One way to do this is with the Resource Manager.

Click on the second cover on the top row and then go to Document->Resource Manager in the top menu.

Because all of the covers are currently the same, there's only one line showing in the resource manager dialogue box. But we can click on the arrow next to that line and it will expand to show all ten instances of that image in the document. Here are the first four showing:

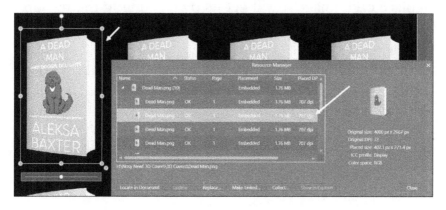

The row that corresponds to the selected image is going to already be highlighted, so just click on Replace and find the second cover that you want to use. Choose Open and Affinity will insert that image into your document in the second cover spot.

Like so:

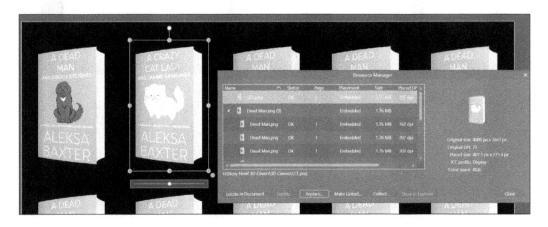

Your other option is to use the Replace Image option in the dynamic menu at the top of the workspace. It should be visible when the Move Tool or Picture Frame Tool are selected.

Click on the cover you want to replace, click on Replace Image, and then navigate to the replacement image and select it.

Repeat until all of the covers have been replaced.

If you insert the wrong image at any point, Ctrl + Z, Undo, or replacing the image with the correct one is probably your best option instead of trying to drag things around to put them in the right location, because if you move any of the picture frames you'll have to realign your images again.

As you replace each image it will get its own listing in the resource manager. Like so:

And there you have it. Once you've swapped out all of the covers, you're done.

Most people won't have ten covers they want to do this way, but the theory remains the same whether it's three covers or twenty. The only issue is visual balance and which of the A+ modules will work best with the number of covers you do have.

I didn't include text here, but for shorter series, you may want to use part of the banner space to do so because it'll give better balance to the use of the space. After we do the ad creatives you should easily be able to make that adjustment.

And remember that what we covered here can work for website banners, Facebook banners, etc. Basically anything that uses a solid background where you want your cover or other images to be displayed. So don't think this is limited to A+ Content.

Okay, then. Now let's put together some advertisements.

BRIEF AD DISCUSSION

Before we do our first ad, though, I want to take a step back and talk advertising in general for a moment.

Amazon AMS ads were the first ads I ever ran where I could get daily sales at full price. They are still my primary advertising spend for non-fiction because of that.

And what's great about AMS is that it's basically your cover driving clicks. No need to also master the art of the two-hundred-word sales pitch or eye-catching ad creatives.

But at some point, especially on the fiction side, AMS ads aren't enough to drive sales. (For me. YMMV.)

Facebook ads, though, if you can master them (and they don't shut down your account repeatedly, ahem), have tremendous potential to generate sales. And not just on Amazon but on all of the sales platforms. They can also be cheaper to run. At least that's been my experience with free runs.

For example, in 2021 I ran a first-in-series title for free for a couple of months at the end of the year. On FB I was able to get around 10 cents a click for my ads, sometimes as low as 6 cents a click. I could get clicks on AMS, too, but they were more like 30 cents a click.

(Now, one could argue that maybe the resultant sales were equivalent because the people on Amazon were already there to buy books whereas the people on FB maybe weren't, so the Amazon downloads were more likely to result in an immediate read and buy of the next book, but for my money I preferred the results from the FB ads.)

Which makes FB ads a tremendous tool to have when you need them.

But one of the problems with running FB ads is that you have to come up with your own advertising images. And that's not an easy thing to do.

I say this based upon the fact that I've sat through a couple years now of one of those high-priced FB advertising courses where people share their ad images. Some do great at coming up with eye-catching ads. Some do not.

(And trust me, I'm not trying to insult anyone here. Sometimes I miss the boat on my ad images, so this is not me looking down on anyone. Hell, you may look at the ones I'm about to show you and think, "Yeah, look who's talking," which, fair enough. But I will point out that the ads I'm going to use here have been profitable for me on Facebook so they're at least successfully reaching *my* particular audience. Or at least a part of it.)

So what makes a good ad?

At a very high level a good ad is one that attracts *your* type of reader and gets them to buy or download your book.

At a more granular level that requires the ad to convey to your target audience that this is something they want.

You do this through the use of text, images, colors, and overall visual appeal.

Which is all a bunch of gobbledy-gook, right? How do you put that into action? It's like "write a good book and it will sell". Okay. How?

The best advice I can give you is to see what others who are successful with running ads in your particular genre are doing, use that to inform your ads, and then experiment until you find something that works for *your* books.

Also keep in mind that selling your book is about alignment. I don't want to divert away from the focus of this book, but I'm going to give you the ten-second version of this lecture.

It is not enough to have a clicky ad. Your ad needs to align with what the potential customer sees on your book product page, too. And, ideally, with the content of the book.

That means your ad, book description, reviews, price, and category listings all have to tell the same story about what the reader is going to get if they download or buy. And if you want them to read more of your books the book itself has to deliver on the promise of the ad and the product page.

I can definitely get a lot of clicks on an ad with a picture of a hot guy. But that does me no good if I'm actually trying to sell a non-fiction book about organizing your closet. (Not unless I make it clear in the ad how those two connect.)

When an ad doesn't perform you need to go down the entire chain.

If you're not getting clicks, what's wrong with the ad image? If you are getting clicks, but no sales or downloads, where's the disconnect between the ad and the product page? If you're getting sales or downloads but no follow through to the next book, what did you promise to readers but fail to deliver?

Or, how did you get them to download, but fail to excite them enough to read? (I have books on my TBR bookcase that have been there for twenty-five years. Why have those books in all those years never quite interested me enough to actually read them?)

Bottom line is you are going to have to experiment to get that all working together. I can't do that for you. What I am doing here is showing you the mechanics of putting together your ads so that you can easily switch them up until you find what works for your books.

Let's get started with our first one, a FB square ad.

FACEBOOK SQUARE AD USING A BACKGROUND IMAGE

Some of my more successful FB ads have been square ones that leverage an image as the background.

In my case these are for my YA fantasy series that has professionally-designed covers. When I changed from the first set of covers that featured a young woman to object-based covers I was able to continue to use the images from my first set of covers as background in my FB ads.

But what we're going to do here can work with any background image, it doesn't have to be an image that comes from your cover. The key, again, is to convey genre and type of story.

Here's the ad I'm going to build:

A quick note here: I did not design either of these covers. I do not have this level of skill. But I can leverage the skill that went into creating these covers in my own ads.

This is an ad I used for a free run for my YA fantasy book in February 2021. The cost per click for this ad set came out at 10 to 11 cents per click with a daily spend set to $10 and it was profitable.

It is a very simple ad. It only has four components: the book cover, the background image, the black space at the bottom, and the text in that black space. That's it.

But hopefully it does what it needs to do. Says this is an ad for a book. That the book is about a young woman. That it's a fantasy novel. Probably fantasy adventure with what looks like a horse and a bow involved. And that they can download it for free if they click on the link.

The beauty of an ad like this is that once you create it, there are an infinite number of variations you can design from this base very quickly.

You can change the book, the background image, the text, the color of the black bar at the bottom. You can move the elements around if you need to.

It shouldn't take more than five minutes to have a new ad once you've built the first one. (Whether that new ad is any good is another question, but the mechanics of swapping elements are not time-consuming.)

So let's go create this now in Affinity.

First step is we need a square canvas that meets the FB ad dimensions. At the time I did this, those were 1080 x 1080.

So, File->New, Web, click on a preset and change it to 1080 x 1080. 72 DPI and RGB/8 should be fine.

Because you might use this more than once, let's create a preset with it. To do that, click on the + sign next to Custom at the top right side of the New Document dialogue box:

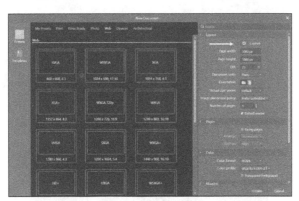

That will add a new preset to the My Presets section that is called Unnamed 1. (Your New Document dialogue box will move you over to that section automatically. The new preset is added at the bottom if you already had presets in there.)

Right-click on the Unnamed 1 thumbnail and choose Rename Preset from the dropdown menu. Type in the name you want for the preset and click OK.

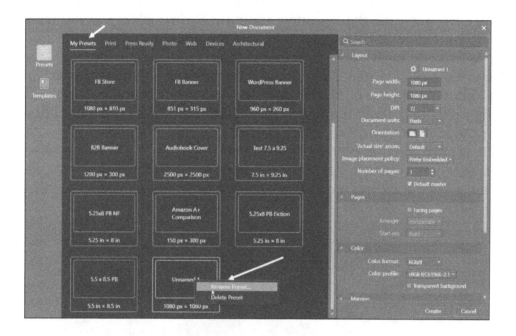

The preset will now show in your My Presets section with whatever name you gave it. For advertising and cover presets I tend to name them based on the place I'm advertising and the type of image it is. The dimensions show below the name, so I don't feel the need to add those in.

In this case I would use FB Square Ad for my name, for example.

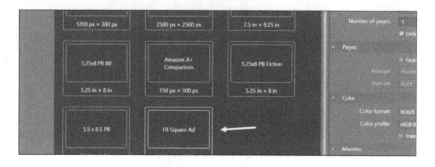

Once that's done and you've selected your preset, click on Create and you should have a nice white square canvas to work on.

* * *

Because I'm in the habit of working with picture frames, the first thing I do is insert a picture frame. So, click on the Picture Frame Rectangle Tool in the left-hand set of icons. (It's the rectangle with an X through it.) Left-click on one corner of your canvas, hold that down, and drag to the opposite corner of your canvas so that you have a picture frame that covers the entire square.

(You could just click and drag to cover the portion of the square where we're going to place the image, but I always draw it to cover the entire canvas. That way if I change my mind about the size or the location of the text element I don't have to also change the size of my picture frame.)

Once you have your picture frame, click on the Place Image Tool icon, navigate to where you have your image stored, and select it. Affinity should bring it into the workspace centered and resized for the size of the frame. Like so:

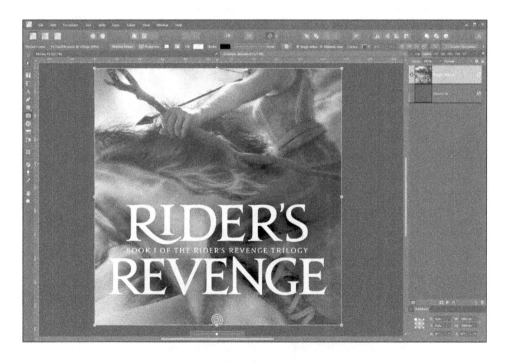

You can see I ended up with the text on the cover in my frame instead of the girl based upon where the center of the cover happened to fall.

I now need to reposition the image until I have the portion of the image I actually want in the picture frame. I can do this by clicking in the center of the arrows on the image in the workspace or by going to the image layer in the Layers studio and then repositioning the image that way.

When working in the image layer, if you click on the Move Tool first before you try to drag the image around it will make doing so easier.

If for some reason you have the text tool selected instead, you'll have to drag from one of the edges of the image to make it work.

(As an aside, when I find that I'm not able to click and move things the way I want or that I'm putting in extra layers I didn't intend to add, it usually boils down to an issue with which tool I have selected on the left-hand side. Usually I can fix a problem like that by clicking on either the Move Tool or the Artistic Text Tool.)

For this particular image, I not only had to drag it downward to focus on the girl on the horse, but I also had to make the image larger by using the slider under the image. I could have also clicked and dragged the image from the corner or used the Transform studio if I'd been in the image layer instead.

Remember that the tools available to you will depend on which layer you're clicked onto in the Layers studio.

Anyway. After a few rounds of moving and resizing the image, I ended up with this:

Much better.

Keep in mind with this that the entire cover imported. I didn't have to take the cover, trim out this part of the image, export that trimmed part to a JPG file, and then import it into my ad. The whole cover is still there. Which means if I decide this is off size-wise or position-wise, I can simply click and drag the image to fix it.

Alright, now it's time to add the text at the bottom.

The first thing I want is the black rectangle that will go in the background. To insert that I click on the Rectangle Tool (the blue filled-in box on the left-hand side set of icons) and then left-click and drag in the workspace to form the shape I want.

Mine inserted as white by default. Here it is:

If you look at the top of your workspace you should see a Fill option with a rounded rectangle next to it that is the same color as the rectangle we just inserted. (The Fill option will always be a rounded rectangle no matter what shape you actually insert.) I have an arrow pointing to it in the image above.

Click on that rectangle. Choose the Swatches tab. Click on the black square swatch at the far left end. This will turn the inserted rectangle black.

(If you didn't want black, this is where you'd choose pretty much any color you want, but for now we're going with black.)

Next I want to insert my text. I could just insert the text directly onto the black rectangle, but I want to put it in a text frame so that I can adjust the width and height of the space I'm centering my text within.

To insert a text frame, I go to the left-hand set of icons and click on the Frame Text Tool, which is the third one down and has a black capital T in a gray box.

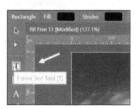

Once I've chosen the Frame Text Tool, I left-click and drag inside the perimeter of the black rectangle I just created to form a smaller rectangle. It shows as a blue border as I create it. Like so:

It doesn't have to be perfect. You can always click on it and drag the edges to adjust it later.

I do want to make sure that the frame is centered in my workspace, though. To do that I go to the Adjustment option up top (the one we used before that looks like a line with two blue bars coming off of the right side) and choose the Align Center option under Align Horizontally.

Now it's time to add my text to the text frame. To do that I click on the Artistic Text Tool on the left-hand side, which is a capital A.

Before I start typing, though, I go to the top of the workspace and click on the black rounded rectangle to change the font color to white. (Otherwise I'll start typing and won't see the text because it will be black on black.)

Remember, the most reliable way to change the color to white is to choose the Swatches tab and then choose the far right swatch which is the white one.

There is no label for that rounded rectangle, but it should be the only one you can see when the text tool is active. It's right next to the U for underline.

Once you've done that, click into the text frame and type your text. For this ad I am using "Download For FREE Today". Initially the text is going to be small and tucked away in the top left corner of the frame, like this:

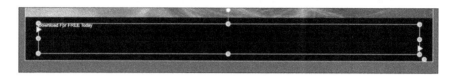

After you've typed in your text (which you can also see in the Layers studio, at least partially), use Ctrl + A to select all of it or highlight it with your mouse.

Next go to the top menu and change the font and font size. I'm using a font called Fontin SmallCaps which is available free for personal and commercial use.

Changing font and font size work just like they do in a standard word processing program. You can click on the arrow next to the current font name or size to see a range of available choices. Either click on the one you want or start typing in the box if you know what you already want.

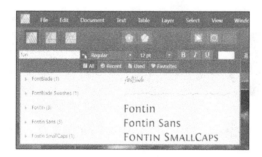

Here I started to type Fontin until I had a shortened list with that font in it and then I clicked on my selection.

If you're not sure what you want to use, you can always hold your mouse over an option to see what it will look like in your document. It will only be applied when you click on it.

I usually change the font first before I change the font size, because some fonts are very different from one another in terms of absolute size at a given point size.

For now I set my font to 72 point because 96 point took it past staying on one line. (If that happens the border around the text will show a red arrow on the right-hand side, indicating that there is additional text that is not currently visible.)

We'll probably come back to this in a minute and customize the point size, but it's a start for now.

Also, while we're still clicked into the text in the text frame we can center our text. Because it is in a text frame, it will center within the frame not within the overall document. This one we have to center differently than the others we've centered because we're centering text not a design element in the layout.

You should be able to see a series of text alignment options on the right-hand side of the dynamic menu above the workspace which is where you already changed the font and font size.

Each alignment option shows a series of lines that form a paragraph. The lines are arranged to show whether it's left-aligned, centered, right-aligned, or justified. You can also hold your mouse over each one to see what it is.

The second option there is to center text. Click on it.

If somehow you clicked away from where you were entering text, it's possible that when you go back to click on that text that Affinity will think you're trying to add a new line of text into your document and will insert a new layer for that.

If that happens (because I do this often), Ctrl + Z to undo the new layer you didn't want, then go to the Layers studio and click on the layer with the text that you wanted to edit first before you click in your workspace where that text is.

Okay, so here we are so far:

I want that text to also be aligned vertically within the text frame. Meaning I want as much space above it as below it in the text frame. (Right now it's top-aligned and you can see more space below the text in the text frame than above it. This is different from the amount of space in the black rectangle behind the text frame. We'll deal with that in a minute.)

To center text vertically within a text frame, use the dropdown option to the right of the horizontal alignment choices we just used. It's going to be the second dropdown option and you want to choose Center Vertically from that dropdown menu.

That will center the text within the text frame. (But not within the rectangle. We'll come back to that in a minute.)

Now it's time to place the three-dimensional book cover.

Once more I like to work with a picture frame. So I go to the Picture Frame Rectangle Tool on the left-hand side of my workspace, click on it, and then left-click and drag in my document to form a rectangle to place my cover within.

When I did this, the layer I created inserted in the Layers studio below my existing layer that had my background image. Which meant that if I went ahead and inserted my cover into the picture frame it wouldn't be visible on my canvas because the picture frame layer was completely covered by my background image.

So let's detour for a second and talk about layers and how they work with one another.

Here is my Layers studio right now:

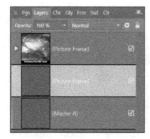

You can see that the top layer has my cover image with the girl on the horse and my text. That is what will be visible in my document no matter what.

The only way to not have that top layer visible would be to reduce the opacity to 0% or to uncheck the box on the right-hand side.

Everything below the top layer will only show if the top layer doesn't cover that portion of the canvas. Since my background image covers the entire space, that means right now nothing below it will show. I need any additional layers I add, like my book cover, to go above the background layer.

So when I add a layer like I just did and it's placed below my background layer, I need to go into the Layers studio and move that layer up. The way to move a layer is to left-click on it and hold that left-click as you drag it to where you want it.

A light blue line will show when you drag your layer to a new location. Release your left-click when that light blue line is where you want the layer to be. (You can see that light blue line in the image below.)

You can also move a layer from being a subset of another layer. For example, when I initially added my rectangle and text those layers both were added in as subsets to the picture frame layer. I don't actually want that necessarily, so what I can do is group the rectangle and text so they can be moved together and then click and drag them up above the background picture frame layer so that they're standalone.

That's what's happening here:

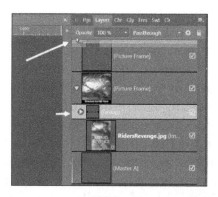

I have the Group layer that's the rectangle and text selected and I've dragged it to the top of my layers and am ready to release my left-click so that it's placed above my book cover picture frame and my background image picture frame.

I probably didn't have to group and move the text, it was visible from where it was, but I did it just to make sure that the text and its background would always be on top of all of the other layers. That way if, for example, my book cover stretched down into the space where I had my text it would do so behind the text, not on top of it.

Here's my new hierarchy:

My text and black rectangle are in a group on top. Below that is my layer for my cover (that I have yet to insert), and below that is my background image. At the very bottom is the Master.

Always check your layer order to make sure that what needs to be on top is. If you swear you added an element and it isn't showing on your final then chances are the layer is too low in the hierarchy so some other element is hiding it or you unchecked the layer and forget to recheck it before you generated your final image.

Okay. I'm going to bring in that book cover now. To do so, I click on the Picture Frame layer for the book cover, then go to the Place Image Tool icon on the left-hand side, click on that, and then I find my 3D cover image and select it.

Affinity should insert the image into the frame at an approximate size that works for the frame, but usually you're going to need to adjust things a bit unless the cover image you're inserting is trimmed down to just the cover which these 3D templates tend not to do. Remember to click down to the actual image layer before trying to move or adjust the image if you do it that way.

(As a side note here, something I've touched upon before is that objects move differently depending on whether you have the Artistic Text Tool or the Move Tool selected on the left-hand side. Generally you can move an object with either one selected, but if you put your mouse over your workspace and see an A next to the cursor then the way to move the object is going to be to left-click on the outer border when you see a black four-sided arrow. Only then will you be able to move the image. If the Move Tool is selected, on the other hand, then you can left-click anywhere on the object to move it. This is something that will occasionally trip me up, so if you're having trouble moving something around, click on the Move Tool black arrow and try again. And, yes, I've said this more than once because it trips me up that often.)

Alright then. Here we are. We have one last thing to do and then we can optimize things.

We need to turn the word FREE yellow. To do so, click on the A for the Artistic Text Tool on the left-hand side and then select the word FREE in your workspace. (Just left-click and drag to highlight.)

There are a couple of ways to change the color of your text. The first is to go to the white colored text rectangle up top in the dynamic toolbar and click on it to bring up the Swatches, Color, and Gradient options.

We already talked about how to use the Swatches option for white, black, and shades of gray as well as recent colors. (Just click over and click on the square for the color you want.)

When it comes to other colors, if you don't need an exact color you can click on the rainbow-shaded color bar at the top of the Hue option to choose a base color and then click anywhere within the rectangle of color below that to choose a specific color. Like so:

That often works for a generic color in a design, especially when working on a screen-based image where you don't have to worry about how it will print. But I find bright yellow a tricky one to get right, so I actually use a specific color for my bright yellow every time.

Which takes us to a different way to apply color.

Instead of clicking on the colored rectangle up top, I go to the Color studio in the top right corner. There I double-click on the circle that shows my current text color. In the screenshot it's a horrid sort of yellow, but yours is probably still white.

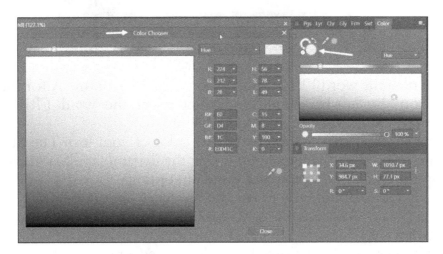

This will bring up the Color Chooser dialogue box where you can input your values for RGB, CMYK, HSL, or the Hex value for the specific color you want. The Hex value for the yellow I like is FFD500, so I type that in the box next to the # sign.

I could also type 255, 213, and 0 in the RGB fields, respectively, to get the same result. That changes the color of yellow for the selected text to the one I like to use.

You may not like that yellow. If you don't, then feel free to experiment around with the color mix for RGB or do a web search to find a specific color code.

Once that's done, this is what we have:

But...

The ad we were trying to replicate is more eye-catching.

The cover was bigger. The background image was closer-up. The text was bigger.

We have the components in the right place, but they don't look as good as they could.

This is why it's always good to experiment with your ad images. Even if you know the components you want to use try variations where you change the size of the elements, change their position, change their colors, etc.

It's fiddly work, but it can make a big difference and as a more novice designer you probably don't yet have the instincts to get the optimal appearance the first time around. I certainly don't. As you can see above.

Now, let me show you a couple tricks.

First, if you ever do want to change the size of a picture frame, like I need to for the book cover component of this ad, you can also resize what's in the frame along with it and save a step.

To do so, click on the Move Tool and then click onto the book cover in the main document. Look for a blue circle *outside of* the main picture frame in the bottom corner. Click and drag on that circle to resize your frame and it will also resize the image at the same time.

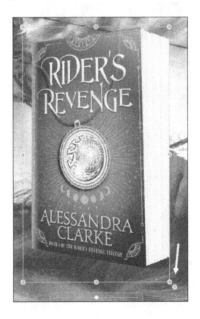

Second, don't forget that you can use the slider under the picture frame to change the size of just the image.

And you can click in the center of the four arrows in the center of the image to move just the image around.

Third, while you can also resize text frames and text together, you need to be careful doing so. It can skew your text in weird ways because it will stretch the text to fit. So if you change the height more than the width that will happen to the text, too. And sometimes the only way to fix it is to delete the text and retype it. (At least as far as I know.)

Okay. On this one, I'm going to resize the black rectangle, expand the text frame, and then bump up the font size for the text. I'm also going to change the background image size and reposition it. And change the book cover size and reposition that.

And here we go.

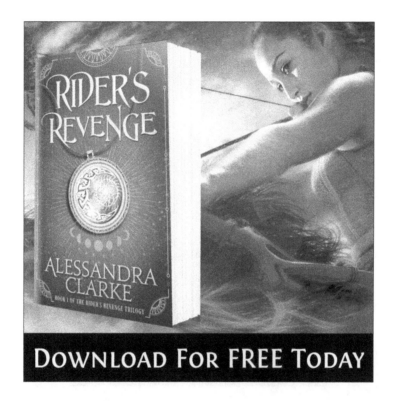

Better. Close to the original we were aiming for and much better than we originally ended with.

Or not

Because one of the nice things you can do with FB ads is have multiple ones running at once. For me aesthetically this ad looks better than the one where everything was smaller, but it's possible that the other image is the better one for selling this book.

And with FB I can run both ads and see which FB prefers and which gets me a lower cost per click and downloads per click.

Now, that probably seemed like a lot of effort for a simple ad. But that's because you're new to doing this. Once you get used to working in Affinity it can take maybe five or ten minutes to put something like that together.

Even better, you can always leverage what you've already done to make it even quicker.

We now have a square ad with download for free today at the bottom, a book cover on the left, and a cover image on the right. I can take that and have a new ad in less than five minutes.

Just to prove that to you I'm going to change this into an ad for book three of the series instead.

First step, I go to Document->Resource Manager and click on each row shown, choose Replace, find a replacement image for it, and select it.

That took maybe a minute to do and this is what I ended up with:

I still need to adjust the image in the background to create an ad that works better for this image, but it'll take me about two minutes.

Here we go:

Fix the text that somehow got out of alignment and we're done in less than five minutes.

In this case, I swapped out both the cover and background image just to show you, but if I was only advertising that first book it takes even less time.

Obviously, the more different the original image and the new image are the more adjustment effort will be involved, but still, it's probably at most ten minutes to create a new ad once you have the components in place.

Definitely save a copy to use later.

Okay. That was FB ad number one. But you could argue that it worked because the covers are expensive covers. So let's do one now with a different layout that uses homemade covers instead. And a "homemade" image, too.

FACEBOOK SQUARE AD USING A SIDE IMAGE

This ad is going to show that you don't need expensive covers to have an effective ad. I ran this ad for my cozy series at the same exact time as I ran the ad above.

The cover is homemade, the book title probably sucks, and the ad image is a random photograph I took of my dog. Granted, she is photogenic, but still. Not ideal elements.

Here it is:

There's even a little bit of orange in the top of that image where I didn't size it correctly. But this ad generated clicks at a cost of 7 to 9 cents a click and resulted in downloads.

Why? Because it makes you stop if you like dogs. And it tells you that it's advertising a book. And that that book is free and has five star reviews from people who loved the dog. The text around the ad image tells you it's a mystery.

And that's really all that's needed. Free. Book. Dog Lovers. Mystery. (Assuming the book delivers on that promise, of course.)

Let's put this thing together. You obviously won't have my cute dog photo to work with, but substitute in your own or a cute kid photo or a hot guy or something that will appeal to your audience.

First things first, File->New, My Presets, FB Square Ad, Create. (Because you saved that as a preset, right? If not, go back to the last chapter for instructions on how to create your square ad to work with.)

Next, Rectangle Tool (the blue square), click and drag over the workspace. Change the color by clicking in the dynamic toolbar up top and using the Swatches tab to select the black square so that your canvas is now black.

After you've done that, click on the Frame Text Tool (the T in a frame) on the left-hand side and click and drag to draw a rectangle at the bottom of the workspace that will fit the review quote you've chosen.

Next, click on the Artistic Text Tool, change your color up top to white, click into the text frame you just created, and type in a dash followed by your review quote. In this case I'm using "I Loved Miss Fancypants!"

Select All (Ctrl + A), change the font and the font size using the dynamic menu up top. Be sure when you choose your font size that you leave enough room to add the five stars at the beginning.

Click back into the text you just added at the start of the text.

Go to the Glyph Browser studio, choose Wingdings from the top menu where the font is listed (remember that you can start typing in the font name to get to that part of the list), and scroll down in the main area of the studio until you see the star shape.

Double-click on it. It should insert into your document where you had your cursor and will also now be at the bottom of the glyph browser studio where your recently-used glyphs are displayed.

You can either go back to your main workspace and highlight and copy the star you inserted (Ctrl + C) and then paste it four more times (Ctrl + V), or you can stay in the Glyph Browser studio and double-click on the star glyph four more times.

Either way you should end up with five stars at the beginning of that line of text.

Readjust the font size or spacing of your text if you need to now that the stars are there, too.

Use the alignment options up top to center your text in the text frame vertically and horizontally. (They're the ones with lines in the dynamic menu in the second row up top that are located to the right of the middle. Vertical alignment is a dropdown menu.)

Once you've done that, you should have something that looks like this:

Now go to the Layers studio, right-click on the text layer, and choose Duplicate. This should create a second text layer directly on top of the first one.

Click onto that duplicate text layer in your workspace and drag upward until your duplicated layer is aligned with the top of the workspace. (Chances are you still have the Artistic Text Tool selected so remember that you can only click and drag from the edge of the layer. Either that or you need to switch over to the Move Tool before you try to move the layer. Also, snapping will let you know when you've dragged your duplicated text layer to the top.)

Next, make sure the Artistic Text Tool is selected and click into the text layer you moved. Delete the stars and the dash. Then delete the rest of the text and replace it with "Download For FREE Today".

(If you delete all of the text at once you'll default to the Wingdings font when you add new text and instead of typing the letter D you'll be typing in a mailbox instead. Which you can do if you want to. Just select all and change the font after you're done.)

Once the new text is added, Select All with Ctrl + A, and change the font size so that the text fills the space as much as possible. Your text should still be centered within its text frame, but if it isn't, fix that, too.

You should now have something like this:

Next step is to color the word FREE and the five stars yellow. Select the word FREE, click on the Color studio tab, double-click the circle for your main color which will likely be white, and type in FFD500 for the color value in the # field (or whatever color value you want to use).

For the five stars you can select them and then either do that again or go to the Swatches studio and click on the yellow-colored swatch from the Recent section. (You can also access Swatches from the colored rectangle in the dynamic menu at the top.)

After you've changed the color of the stars and the word FREE, it's time to add your images.

Click on the Picture Frame Rectangle Tool (looks like a rectangle with an X on it) in the left-hand side set of icons, and then click and drag to draw a rectangle in your workspace that stretches between the two text frames and is 360 pixels wide. (Using the rule of thirds, we divide 1080 by three to get 360.)

As you align the picture frame with the edges of the text frames and of the master you should see the red and green snapping lines to tell you you've aligned with the edges

Next, place your three-dimensional cover in the picture frame by clicking on the Place Image Tool (landscape image on the left-hand side) and selecting your cover from where you have it saved.

Once the cover has been inserted, adjust the image so that it's fully visible and centered in the frame.

You should now have something like this:

Add another picture frame that covers the remaining area. I actually made mine 693 not 720 because I thought 720 would crowd the book cover too much.

Insert your chosen image and adjust to fit the frame.

In my case, the picture came in sideways, so let's discuss how you can fix that.

Option one is to click and drag on the white circle at the top of the perimeter of the image. As you hold your left-click and drag, the image should rotate with your mouse.

Here you can see the image in mid-rotation. I have an arrow pointing at the white circle:

Another option is to change the R value in the Transform studio. In this case a -90 degrees worked to change the orientation.

If you use the Transform option, it may move the image to a location outside of the picture frame, and you'll have to drag it back into frame.

As you work to position your image, Affinity should provide green or red alignment lines for the alignment of the image within the picture frame. Here, for example, the image is centered in the frame so there is a green line showing down the center of the picture frame:

The problem with relying on these lines is that Affinity is using the entire image, and the center of the image may not actually be the center of the part of the image that you want to emphasize.

For example, here the dog is off-center of the frame even though the overall picture is centered. I don't want that much of the background bookcase to show on the right-hand side of the picture frame so I need to adjust manually instead.

When I do that, here is our final version:

(And I can attest that even though it's slightly off from the original, it still works just fine because I uploaded it to FB after I created it and it gave me 6 cent clicks the first day.)

* * *

Very basic, right? But it gets the point across. Do you love dogs? Then look, free. Book. Five stars.

The other ad that ran at the same time and did just as well was this one:

It does the exact same thing. Look, dog. Free. Book. Five stars. And because these are cozies, bright colors work.

Again, once you create one of these it's a very simple matter to swap out a book or an image or a quote to get a new ad image.

* * *

One more thought about these two ads we just did.

I personally prefer to put my text on a solid background because it's easier for someone viewing the ad to see what the text says. But I've seen successful ads that didn't set the text apart like that.

Although the ones that put text on a textured background still tend to mute the background enough that the text is the main component of that part of the image.

The key is to experiment and see what works for your books and your audience.

* * *

Okay. So far what we've done has been very basic. We haven't manipulated any images at all, we've just brought them into Affinity. We've basically been building with pre-formatted puzzle pieces.

But now let's experiment a bit and bring in images that we manipulate. To shake things up, I'm going to do this one as a BookBub CPC ad but what we're going to do will work for any ad image you want to create. The key is to keep in mind proportion and balance for each ad size.

BOOKBUB AD WITH IMAGE ADJUSTMENTS AND 99 CENT LABEL

Originally I was going to use another FB ad for this chapter, but I just looked at a few of my old ad images and decided they weren't very good so I didn't want to use them. And that's something you're going to have to accept as you learn to do your own ads. Sometimes you think you did a good job with something, but you really didn't. And worse, sometimes you don't realize it until you look back later. So there you were, out in public, looking bad.

But this entire industry—including the writing—is about taking your hits, learning from them, and improving for the next go round.

So I'm going to do something risky here and we're just going to build an ad from scratch. Which means that three months from now I might flip through this book and think, "Wow, that was an ugly ad image, why on earth did I use that in that book?"

It happens. But no matter how bad the ad we're about to create turns out, at least you'll learn the additional skills I wanted to show you and you can do a better job with your own ads.

Here goes.

According to their FAQs BookBub CPC ads need to be 300 x 250 pixels. So File->New, Web, 300 width, 250 height, 72 DPI is fine, landscape orientation, RGB/8. Feel free to turn this into a preset that you save in your My Presets section for future use. If not, just click Create.

You should now have a big white almost-square rectangle to work with.

I'm going to use my fantasy cover for this one (because it's more forgiving) and I actually want to use the colors from the cover in the rest of my ad, so the first thing I'm going to do is bring in the cover.

Picture Frame Rectangle Tool. Add the cover with the Place Image Tool. Adjust to fit.

Here we go with a picture frame that is 150 W by 235 H:

Now, the reason I brought in the cover first is because I don't want to use black this time. I want to tie into the colors in that cover. So my next step is going to be to add a rectangular space at the bottom (using the Rectangle Tool) and to color that rectangle a color that corresponds to the cover.

First things first, I move the cover up a bit and then use the Rectangle Tool to click and drag my rectangle into place at the bottom.

To use the color from the cover, I go to the Color studio and left-click on the eyedropper and then hold down that click as I move my mouse over my cover. You can see the circle that surrounds my mouse as I do this.

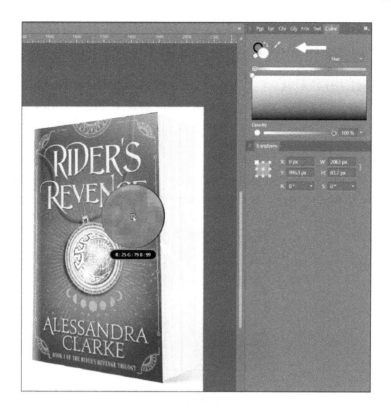

Also, the color in the circle next to the eyedropper up in the Color studio will change to reflect my currently selected color.

Once I have a color I like, I can just let up on the left-click to choose it. (You can see that the color on this cover is not uniformly one color so I have a range of options to choose from. With some of my other covers where I used a solid fill for the background I'd just have one single option.)

That chose the color for me, but to actually use it I need to double-click on the colored circle next to the eyedropper in the Color studio. That will make it my main color and also should apply it to my rectangle at the same time.

(The only reason it wouldn't is if you had the border option instead of the main color option selected for some reason. Remember the main color is the solid circle, the border color is the doughnut and whichever is on top is the one you're working with in the Color studio.)

Once you select the color it will also be available in your Swatches studio under Recent in case you need it again.

Okay. Next I want to add text to my rectangle. In this case I'm going to use some bulleted descriptions separated by a moon glyph which fits the theme of the cover and the book.

I'm not going to put this one into a text frame, so I just click onto the A for the Artistic Text Tool on the left-hand side of the workspace and then click onto my ad and start to type.

My text is "MEDDLING GODS HIDDEN CONSPIRACIES ENEMIES AS ALLIES." I'm going to use a font on this called Desire because that will go well with the cover text.

I use Ctrl + A to select all and then change the font and font size up top in the font dropdowns.

I also want to change the color of my text, so next I click on the black rectangle for the color option in that same row.

And once more I'm going to use a color from the cover. So I left-click on the eyedropper and hold that left-click until I take the color for my text from the cover. To apply it to my text, I double-click on the circle next to the eyedropper once it has a color showing.

Now it's time to add the moon symbols that I'm going to use between the descriptive phrases.

First step, I click back into my text after the word GODS, add a space, and then go to the Glyph Browser studio.

I want the Wingdings 2 font and then the quarter moon symbol that's after the numbers but before the clocks. I double-click to insert into my text. I do the same after the word CONSPIRACIES.

Be sure to add the extra space *before* you add the symbol because if you add the space after you add the symbol it may be a different sized space and that will make your text look uneven. (Ask me how I know. Ctrl + Z, Undo, is my best friend.)

At this point I adjust the font size again if I need to. I prefer to select all and manually change the font size in the dynamic menu at the top, but you can also click and drag on the box around the text to resize everything that way. Just be careful, because sometimes it will stretch out the text in weird ways if you do that.

To center the text element in your workspace, click on that layer in the Layers studio, and then use the Alignment option in the top row (the one with the line and two blue bars) and choose Align Center from the Align Horizontally section.

Here's what I get after that's all done:

I'm not sure that text at the bottom is bright enough. I took it from the full moon on the cover, but I think I want to change that out for the brighter color in the author name. So let me do that now. I go back and select all the text by clicking on my text layer in the Layers studio, making sure my A is clicked on in the left-hand set of icons, and then clicking into my text.

Ctrl + A to select all.

Next I click on the text color in the dynamic menu up top, click on the eyedropper and hold as I select my new color, and then double-click on that circle next to the eyedropper to apply it.

Better.

(And if I didn't like it and decided the first color was better I have the option to Undo. Or I can go to the Swatches panel and click on the old color from there because it was used in the document so should be available to select there until I close the file. And if neither one is right, I can try again to get a color from the cover that I think works better. Or start clicking around for nearby color options in one of the color dropdowns.)

Okay.

Time to bring in an image for the background. I could use my original cover, but I'm going to actually use a stock photo for this. And we'll do this one without a picture frame for now, too, just so you can see how that works.

So, go to the Layers studio, click on the Master A layer, then click on the Place Image Tool, and find the image you want. Select it and then click and drag to insert.

Here we go.

This was an image of a desert city, but the city is currently hidden behind the cover.

And the image doesn't currently fit the entire space. I can click and drag the image to make it bigger, but I don't want to. I want that city to be near to the size it is now. It needs to attract attention, but not too much attention.

Which means I need to find a way to fill that extra white space that the image doesn't cover. But before we deal with that, I want to flip my image so we can see the city on the left-hand side of the ad.

I do that by going to Layer->Transform->Flip Horizontal.

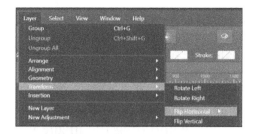

If you ever flip an image like this—and I find it can be handy to do at times—the next thing you need to do is make sure that the image still works. Was there any text in the image that is now backwards or upside down? (If you flip vertically.) Does the perspective look skewed now? Does it just seem off?

Also, if you flip an image like I just did here and then use the resource manager to replace the image, the new image will also be flipped. And any transformations you applied to the image will also be applied to the new one.

This has messed me up a few times, so it's worth mentioning. If you're going to do a lot of image manipulation on one image but not others for an ad, you might want to save a clean version of your file first before you start that manipulation work. (You can at least turn off a lot of effects in the Layers studio, though, if you don't do that.)

Anyway. My image is now flipped, but it's still not covering the whole space.

I can fix some of that with resizing.

Because I am not working in a picture frame, if I resize the image beyond the borders of my ad the image will be fully visible in my workspace even though it won't appear in the final ad I create. Like you can see here where my Pages studio shows what the ad would actually look like but the workspace shows the full image going beyond the boundaries of my canvas:

The background image you can see above has gone beyond the perimeter of the ad on the right-hand side as well as the bottom.

I personally find it a challenge to work with an image like this because it makes it harder to properly balance my different elements when what I can see on the screen is not what will appear in the ad. This is why I usually use picture frames.

And if I were going to keep this image at the larger size I have it at right now, I'd probably add a picture frame and drag the image into the frame to eliminate that issue.

But we're going to do something different here. We're going to duplicate this image layer, flip it back to the original orientation, and then line the edges of the two images up. Since the merge line will be hidden behind the cover this is a quick and dirty way for us to fill in that last little bit of white space in a way that matches the rest of the image.

It's not something I'd recommend where details really matter (like in the center of a cover), but for something like this that's going to be in the background behind another element it should work.

First step, click on the image layer in the Layers studio, right-click, Duplicate. Next, Layer->Transform->Flip Horizontal. Finally, click and drag on the new layer until you see the green line that shows the old and new layer are touching but not overlapping.

You also want the red lines at top and bottom to show they're aligned that way as well.

A way to confirm that the images are aligned top to bottom is to click on each layer and look at the Y value in the Transform studio. They should be the same.

If I think I might change the size of the background layer or move it around more, then I can select both layers now and group them so that they will move together or resize together. (Click on one layer in the Layers studio, hold down Ctrl and click on the other, then Ctrl + G or right-click and choose Group from the dropdown to group them.)

A note here that if you had these two layers in a picture frame sometimes weird things can happen when you group them. But for this, they should be fine.

So where are we at the moment? If I export this right now, this is what we have.

Which is fine. Not great. Not, wow I want that book right now, but it might be good enough to get clicks.

Let's try something to make it pop more. I'm going to put in lines to divide this space in thirds and see where they fall.

But first, the image falling outside of the workspace now that I've duplicated it is throwing my eye off, so I am going to go ahead and add a picture frame and drag the background image into it.

To add the picture frame, I go to Picture Frame Rectangle Tool, click and drag to add it and then move the edges of the frame until it aligns along the edges of my canvas. (Sometimes when you have elements already in your design it's easier to click further inside or even outside the edges of the canvas and create a frame and then drag the edges of the frame to the perimeter after that.)

Once I have my frame I go to the Layers studio, left-click on my grouped background images, and drag that group to the new picture frame layer.

Sometimes when you do this, the layer you dragged into the frame will disappear, so you have to be careful what part of the picture frame layer you drag onto. Try dragging to the left-hand side to get it to nest properly.

The background images should be added in as a subset of the picture frame. Like so:

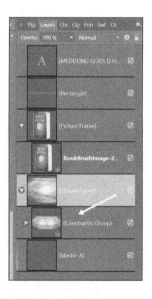

That's much easier to work with for me. Nice clean edges that don't go past the edge of my canvas.

Also, be sure that the picture frame layer for the background is the layer just above your Master A layer so that it truly is in the background. You don't want it to cover one of your other elements.

Okay. Now that we've cleaned things up, let's divide this space into thirds.

We have a width of 300, so that's going to be 100 and 200 where we need our guide lines. For the height we start with 250, but the rectangle I added is 24.3 so let's say 25, that gives me 225, divide by three and we get 75 so we need guide lines at 75 and 150.

The way to place a guide line is to left-click on the ruler on the side or the top of the black area in your workspace and then drag into your image.

As you drag you should see a light blue line and a small box that shows the X or Y location of your line. So in this picture it's a little hard to see but I've dragged my guide line 200 pixels into the document.

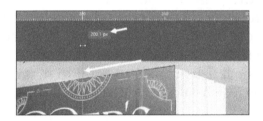

For a vertical line you drag from the side. For a horizontal line you drag from the top. If you need to adjust the placement of a line after the fact, left-click on it and drag. (You may need to click on the Move Tool first to be able to left-click on the line.)

Here is my document now with guide lines for the thirds.

So what do we do with this?

Unfortunately these elements aren't in great spots. That power position in the top left third is empty sky. But the city does fit nicely in the second third on the left side. And our main element in the book cover is falling fairly nicely onto the right-hand third line and then in the center third section.

I could increase the size of the city to fall more into that power position, but then I move the emphasis from the book cover to the city and we don't want that. But I can move the image up a bit to align the line within the city to the second horizontal blue line we inserted.

And maybe I can bump up the background image size a bit. Now that we have the two images joined, it's a little harder to click and drag from a corner, so I'm going to click on the grouped image layer and use the Transform studio instead.

Before I change either the H or W values for the image in the Transform studio, though, I need to be sure to click on the two little circles with a line between them to the right of the W and H value fields to Lock Aspect Ratio.

You lock the aspect ratio so that the width and height of the element adjust together. This keeps the image from becoming skewed. It doesn't matter with a solid background or a frame, but it matters very much with any image you work with.

And now we experiment resizing and adjusting our elements to get them to work the best together while keeping the emphasis on the book cover.

You can zoom in or out on your workspace using View->Zoom and then choosing from the options there. (Since this is a smaller image, zooming to 100% actually makes it pretty tiny.)

After some back and forth, here's where I ended up.

Note that the city is now sitting along the second horizontal line. And that the text of Revenge in the cover is sitting along the first. And that the central image in the cover is resting upon the second horizontal line and mostly at the intersection with the second vertical line. The E in Rider's is also now on the second vertical line.

Is it perfect? No. But I think at this point it would serve its purpose. The eye is drawn to the cover. The image in the background conveys the setting. The text along the bottom adds more information if people want it.

It's not the best ad ever. But it would probably generate clicks and sales.

Since we're here, though, let's talk about some other things you could do to that background image. (For those of you reading this in black and white what we're about to do may not look all that different and for that I apologize. You can do this on your screen as you read along to see what happens.)

Okay.

Go to the Layers studio and click on the background image under the picture frame and then go down to the bottom and click on the little icon that's a half-filled circled. If you hold your mouse over it, it's called Adjustments.

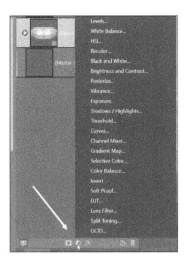

Right next to it is an *fx* icon that's called Layer Effects that will open a Layer Effects dialogue box for you.

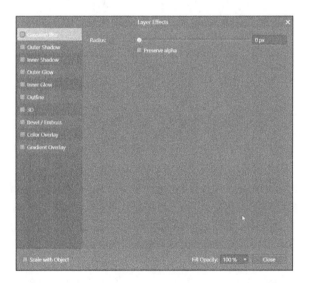

These are the two places where most of the adjustments you can make in Affinity Publisher are located. (Photo as I mentioned before has a lot more that you can do.) You can also access these through the Layer->New Adjustment and Layer->Layer Effects options in the top menu.

Most of these options we're not going to cover here, but feel free to experiment with them.

The one that I want to show you now is an effect that makes an image black and white.

Go to Layer->New Adjustment->Black and White up top or right-click on the Adjustments option I just showed you and then choose Black and White from the dropdown menu.

That will immediately turn the image black and white. It will also give you a Black and White dialogue box where you can adjust how different colors in the image are converted to black and white.

The image I'm using is mostly pinks and oranges, so adjusting the slider for blue doesn't really change anything, but using the red or magenta sliders definitely does.

That Blend Mode dropdown at the bottom can give you all sorts of interesting effects, but if what you want is just a basic black and white image, then keep it on Normal.

We can then add on top of that a Color Overlay to create a sepia-like appearance. First, make sure the layer is selected in your Layers studio and then open the Layer Effects dialogue box. (The little *fx* icon I mentioned above or go to Layer->Layer Effects to bring up the Layer Effects dialogue box.)

Click the checkbox for Color Overlay and then click on the words Color Overlay. That should turn the entire image black or whatever the color showing for color overlay is.

The Color Overlay settings should look like this:

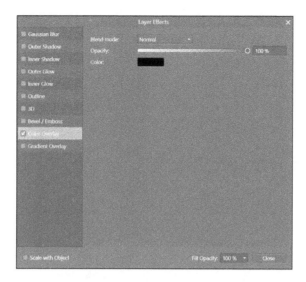

(The Layer Effects dialogue box can be weird sometimes because you can check a box for an effect but it doesn't actually take you to the settings for that effect when you do so, so be sure to click on the effect name to bring up the settings.)

To see the image under the overlay, you need to change the Opacity setting. You can either type in a value, or left-click on the circle and drag along the slider until you like what you see.

Before I do that, though, I'm going to click on the black rectangle next to Color, go to my Swatches option in the dropdown menu, and change the color. I'm going to try using the color that I pulled from the moon.

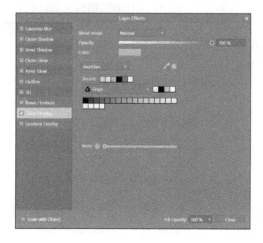

With my opacity at 45% here is my ad:

That bright pink and orange image is now a sort of muted beige in the background and the cover is definitely the focus.

Is that better than the colored version? Eh, I don't know. The color pulls the eye better, but maybe it muddies things up for a viewer and they don't know where to focus their attention.

But that's the beauty of CPC ads. You can put up a lot of variations and see which ones turn out to be the most clickable. (Just be sure you're also looking for sales or downloads, too. Clicks without purchases are just money spent.)

One more thing to mention on these effects. They are non-destructive, meaning you have not changed the underlying image. You can remove them easily by unchecking their box.

For the black and white adjustment, it's done in the Layers studio.

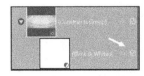

For the Color Overlay it's done by opening the Layer Effects dialogue box and unchecking the adjustment from there.

So don't be afraid to experiment with different adjustments. You can also delete the ones in the Layers studio. Just click on the white image portion of the layer to make sure you've selected that layer and then right-click, Delete from the dropdown.

One last thing we need to cover and that's how to add an element to your ad that says either "Free" or "99 Cents" or something like that.

The first thing we need is to click on the Rectangle Tool, but this time I'm going to click on the white arrow in the corner to see the full list of options, and I want to choose the Star Tool.

I can draw a star using the Star Tool just like I drew a rectangle with the Rectangle tool: left-click and drag on the canvas.

If you drag at an angle, it should stay proportionate. Here is my first attempt:

I think I actually want it more squat than that so I'm going to resize from the bottom a bit. To do so I just left-click and drag on that blue circle on the bottom border.

Next step is to click on the A for the Artistic Text Tool and type whatever it is you want, "Free", "99 Cents", etc. If you want to use the actual cents sign, use the Glyph Browser studio for that.

You can click on your text layer and then click and drag from the corner to resize the text to fit neatly into the star. Or you can always just change the font size in the dynamic menu up top until it fits well.

I like to position the text layer on top of the star so that it mostly fills the interior and is centered nicely. Here's what I ended up with:

My star background defaulted to the background I'd used for the rectangle at the bottom of the screen and the text color I'd used for the text I added down there. It blends well, but maybe I don't want it to blend. Maybe I want it to stand out strongly as the primary reason to click.

If that's the case then I should click on my star layer in the Layers studio, go to the Color studio, and change my color over to something like my bright yellow. Which then requires selecting the text and changing it to a different color as well, maybe a bright blue since that's the color on the opposite side of the color wheel from the yellow I'm using.

At this point, I go to the Layers studio, select the text and star layers, and group them so that they stay together and I don't have to reposition my text on my star if I move things around or resize them.

Now it's time to decide where you want your star and how big you want it to be.

I tend to prefer to put anything like this in touch with the cover, so I'm going to put it on my first horizontal dividing line, but not at that power point that's the intersection with the first vertical dividing line.

Also, I think I want the colored background instead of the muted one if I'm going to use a bright yellow star, so let me do that as well. And this is what I get.

I'm not sure the star adds to the image, but I'd try it and see what the results were.

Looking at this now as I edit this book there are some more tweaks I would probably make. I'm not sure I like the moon symbols for my dividers and if I did keep the star with free on it I might try moving it around. But it probably works okay. And there's only so much time you can spend on something like this before you just have to give it a try and see if it gets you profitable sales.

EXPORT, SAVE, AND MORE

Before we wrap up, just a few more things you need to know.

EXPORT

To take the finished image you've designed and export it for upload to your chosen advertising platform, go to File->Export in the top menu.

This should bring up the Export Settings dialogue box.

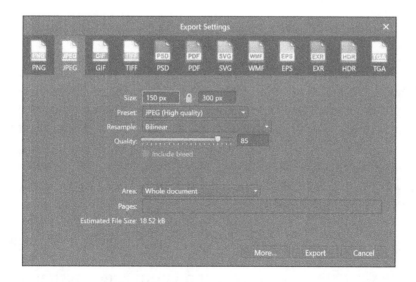

For the images we dealt with in this book you're going to want to click on the JPEG icon in the top row of choices.

I usually set my quality to 85% or so. (I used to set it 100% but setting it lower saves on file size and doesn't appear to have a strong impact on the image quality. I ran into a few sites that rejected my files as too big when the setting was at 100%.)

For Area you want the whole document and you don't need any special settings or to change the default preset.

Once you're ready, click Export. Choose your file location, verify the file name or assign a file name, and save.

Be certain that your file is exporting where you want it to. Mine defaults to wherever I exported to last and this sometimes gets me in trouble if I work on more than one project in a day. So always double-check before you export.

As you can see in that screenshot, there are a number of other file types you can choose for your export, but I believe JPEG should work for all advertising options.

I do use PNG when I have to export an image with a transparent background such as a three-dimensional cover. I leave all of the settings as is so it's just a matter of clicking on PNG up top in the dialogue box.

TIFF images are what you should use if you're creating a print interior.

PDF are required for print covers, but I cover that in *Affinity Publisher for Basic Book Covers*. If you need to export to PDF for a print cover and haven't read that book just keep in mind that Amazon's template includes bleed, but Ingram's does not. So check that box accordingly.

PREFLIGHT

There are times when File->Export will not bring up the Export Settings dialogue box. Instead you will get an error message that says, "Preflight Warnings: Your document has unresolved preflight errors." This happens all the time with print interiors, but is generally more rare when dealing with advertising images.

When it has happened to me it is usually because one of the images in my ad is below the DPI that I set for the file. It can also be because you scaled an image and didn't keep it proportional.

If you choose to Open Preflight, Affinity will open the Preflight studio which will include any issues in the document. Like here where it is telling me I have one image in my file where the DPI is too low, which means it may be blurry, and that I have one where the scaling was not proportionate which means the image may look "off".

If the final product looks fine to you, because we're working on a computer screen and your end viewer will also be on a screen, you can probably just ignore the preflight issues and continue.

But I created this error and I can see on my screen that the low DPI one would need to be fixed. It's bad enough that I can't tell what the image is supposed to be.

If you double-click on the error in the preflight studio, it should highlight the layer with the problem.

Both of these issues can be fixed using the Transform studio to change the image dimensions.

For the low DPI image you can scale the image until the error message goes away, so reduce H or W with Lock Aspect Ratio turned on until the message disappears.

For the non-proportional scaling, Shift and double-clicking on one of the side borders will return the image to a proportionate size.

Or sometimes I just turn *off* Lock Aspect Ratio and then adjust either H or W until that message disappears.

With either of these errors, you will need to reevaluate your final image to make sure it didn't mess anything up when you fixed that component.

Your other option when that error appears is to simply ignore and continue your export. If things look good to you and it's for an online image, then do so. But take an extra careful look at your final product to be sure.

If it's for print, DO NOT trust what you see on the screen. Print a physical copy for review. Something can look clear on screen but be blurry printed.

SAVE

To save your Affinity file go to File->Save, choose your location and name for your Affinity file, and then click on Save. Ctrl + S also works.

LINKED IMAGES

Be careful if you later move where you have the images you used to create your ad saved. If the files were linked instead of embedded, the next time you open your file, Affinity will tell you that it can't find those images and will give you an opportunity to identify the new location for the images. If you don't provide a new location for the image(s) it will export a blurred image in place of the images it can't find.

This should be pretty obvious for an ad like the ones we've discussed, because everything is right there for you to see. (It's sometimes harder to catch in a print book with lots of images.)

If you notice a blurred image but Affinity didn't ask you to replace it, go into the Resource Manager, find the entry for that image, and use Replace to tell Affinity the new location for the image.

WRAP-UP

Okay, so that's basically how to put together images for ads or websites, etc. in Affinity Publisher. Other than the three-dimensional cover issue, Publisher is more than sufficient to let you put together any advertising image you need.

Just remember what your goal is in creating any sort of ad image. And that's to attract your type of reader and get them to buy or download your book. (Or sign up for your newsletter if that's your goal.) You want your type of person to act.

So with everything you do, ask "will this attract my readers and will they act if it does?" If not, fix it.

And, yes, I'm well aware that's easier said than done. I've been at this a number of years and I'm still not sure I know who my type of reader is for anything I write. So sometimes it's a matter of shooting blind and then judging the results and then adjusting and trying again.

For example, I had a FB ad that did very well at getting readers of George RR Martin to click. But they didn't buy. So they weren't my readers. Or if they were, something on my book page turned them away.

I've also had AMS ads that did very well at getting Sarah J. Maas readers to buy the first book in my fantasy series. But if my also-boughts can be believed, they didn't go on to buy book two so they weren't really my readers. They were fantasy readers, but I didn't give them what they wanted for them to continue reading my books.

So an ad and its visible performance (clicks) is just the beginning. You have to then figure out if that ad really brought in *your* readers.

Okay? Make sense?

The Appendix, as I mentioned before, has quick takes for everything we covered here. So if you want to use one of these skills like, Add a Picture Frame, you don't have to reread that whole section, just check the Appendix.

Also, there is a video version of this course available on Teachable at https:/ /ml-humphrey.teachable.com/courses. Use code MLH50 to get fifty percent off of the cost of the course.

And if you enjoyed this book and want to continue to expand your image design skills using Affinity Publisher then check out *Affinity Publisher for Basic Book Covers* where I will walk you through how to design some basic covers as well as how to take an ebook cover and create print covers for KDP paperback, IngramSpark paperback, and IngramSpark hard cover.

Alrighty then. Good luck with it. Reach out if you get stuck.

Affinity Publisher for Basic Book Covers

Affinity Publisher for
Self-Publishing - Book 3

M.L. HUMPHREY

CONTENTS

INTRODUCTION

In *Affinity Publisher for Ad Creatives* we walked through some basic tools that you can use to put together images for Amazon A+ Content, website banners, Facebook ads, BookBub ads, etc.

I want to continue what we started there and now show you how to do some basic ebook covers as well as how to take an existing ebook cover and turn it into a simple paperback or hard cover.

Specifically, we are going to walk through how to:

- Create two ebook covers that use a single image and solid-colored background for the title text

- Create an ebook cover that uses a single image for the entire background

- Create a paperback print cover for use on Amazon using a solid colored background

- Create a paperback print cover for use on IngramSpark using a solid colored background

- Create a case laminate hard cover for use on IngramSpark using a solid colored background

I want to remind you that these books use Affinity Publisher not Affinity Photo.

Even though Publisher isn't the best Affinity program for advanced cover design, it actually works very well for simple design projects like the ones we're going to cover in this book.

And I personally prefer to work in Affinity Publisher because I'm already working with it for my interior book layouts so I don't have to relearn how to perform a task, such as placing an image, that works in a slightly different way in Affinity Photo. (But ultimately if you do want to start combining images and doing more advanced covers, that's where you'll need to go. Plenty of tutorials that work for Photoshop will also work for Affinity Photo.)

Alright. Moving on.

Many of the tools we will use here are the same ones we used for ad creatives, but we're also going to use a few more tools and techniques and broaden our use of the tools you already learned.

(If you didn't read the book on ad creatives, you should still be okay, just know that the books were written to flow from one to the next so I might cover things a little faster this time around, but there's always the Appendix for the thirty-second version of how to do everything I mention in case you feel a little lost.)

Once again, I also want to reiterate that I am not a graphic design professional. No one is going to be paying me $600 for a cover anytime soon. What we are going to create here are *basic* covers. They get the job done, but we're not going to be doing image-blending or mask layers or any of that fun stuff that can really take covers to a different level.

This is just the basics. Taught by a self-published author who doesn't have enough patience to wait six months for a cover or the funds to pay for covers for short stories that may only sell ten copies.

Now, having said that, I do think that the skills you'll learn here are absolutely of value and that I can teach them to you.

So without further ado, let's dive in on some design principles. I'm going to reiterate what we covered in the ad creatives book, but also add some detail around print versus screen colors, element legibility, and fonts.

DESIGN PRINCIPLES

COLOR

RECAP

As a reminder, each genre or category of book has its own color scheme. As a good example, look at the difference between dark romance and sweet romance. Even without the other cover elements involved, you can usually tell a dark romance from a sweet romance on color scheme alone.

Which means the first rule for any cover design is to know where your book fits and to use the colors that apply to books like yours. Keep in mind when doing this research that miscategorizing of books is fairly rampant on Amazon, so you really do need to know who writes what you write.

Colors can also have cultural meanings and feelings associated with them. A bright red is different from a pale yellow in terms of what it conveys to the viewer.

When in doubt, choose complementary colors. These are ones that sit opposite one another on the color wheel.

Contrast is also good. This is why you see so much black on white, white on black in ordinary signage. Because the more contrast there is between text and background the more likely it is someone can read the text.

Okay, now on to the new information with respect to color:

PRINT VS SCREEN COLORS

As a recap, the way that color is created on a computer or phone screen (using light) is different from the way that color is created when it's printed (using ink). For computers, the colors are RGB colors. For print, the colors are CMYK colors.

What this means for you in Affinity is that for print you should set your project up to use CMYK so that you're seeing a more true version of what the project will look like when you actually print. But still, the best thing to do is to actually print out your paperback cover. Do not trust what you see on the screen.

And if you are unsure of your colors, definitely order a proof copy. I once had a cover that looked like it was red on the screen, but it printed bright pink. Which was not good because the target audience was men who would not be drawn to a pink cover.

Personally I've not had issues with blues or blacks, but I have definitely seen variety in bright green and red.

Now, some people will adjust their print covers to make them as close to their ebook covers as possible and you can definitely try to do so. I personally tend to leave my print covers unadjusted and simply accept that my print covers will come out darker.

Because I'm using simple designs, this isn't generally a big issue. If you're using complex images, like in an illustrated cover, it can be a bigger problem because an image that looked fine on the screen can look muddy when printed.

So definitely order a print proof if you get that fancy. (And print it off on your printer first. It's possible you'll see you have issues without having to waste the time and money to get that print proof in the mail.)

Also, keep in mind that even if you adjust your print cover so that it will look good when it prints, the thumbnail version available on vendor websites that readers look at to decide whether or not to buy your book is still going to be displayed electronically using RGB colors.

Okay, now let's talk about element placement and legibility.

ELEMENT PLACEMENT AND LEGIBILITY

RECAP

Remember the rule of thirds as well as the golden ratio.

The rule of thirds is where you split the area you're working with into thirds both horizontally and vertically and try to place key elements of your design either within those sections or at the power points where the lines intersect.

The golden ratio of 1:1.618 can be another design approach to work with either with elements in an image or to determine the relative size of different text elements. So, for example, series name is in X pt size and title is in 1.618 times X pt size.

Also, keep in mind that for most self-published authors, even your print sales will happen online. So subtlety isn't going to help you. Your cover needs to work in thumbnail size on a page with probably a dozen other covers trying to draw your buyer's attention.

ELEMENT LEGIBILITY

Let's expand on that issue of legibility for a minute.

I often see people talk about some really cool thing they're doing with their print cover. Like a really subtle pattern that will look so cool up close. Which could be a nice little bonus for a reader who buys the print book.

But if that cool, subtle pattern makes for a confusing and muddied thumbnail? That's a fail. Because the customer is never going to order the book and see the cool little detail.

(It's like the person who says their book gets really interesting in Chapter 10. If readers put down the book before Chapter 10 because they're bored, that great twist does not matter. It has to draw them in up front and keep them reading until Chapter 10.)

Another issue I've seen is images that are too complicated for a thumbnail view. I think this issue stems from trying to model covers off of trade-published books, which at least historically are much more likely to be bought in a bookstore. As a self-published author, always be looking at your book cover in thumbnail before you finalize it.

It has to work at that tiny size. Print or ebook, it doesn't matter.

If your cover doesn't attract your reader in that little thumbnail size on Amazon, it's not an effective cover.

FONT

RECAP

Your choice of font is incredibly important. As important as any image on your cover. Look at other books in your category to see what kinds of fonts are being used for your type of book.

You don't need to know the entire history of fonts, but do know that there are main categories of font, like serif vs. sans-serif, and that some fonts have a very heavy history that can skew perceptions for those who know that font. Think Comic Sans as a good example.

Once more we have the issue of the thumbnail. But when we're dealing with a cover it's possible that the legibility of the title and author name are secondary to the main image on the cover, especially if that image is a dragon (for fantasy) or a shirtless man (for high-heat romance), for example.

HIERARCHY

Let's expand on the issue of hierarchy when it comes to fonts. Generally, the more important elements on your cover should be in a larger font size than the less important elements.

So your title should be a larger font size than your series name, for example. And your series name should probably be a larger font size than your review quotes, if you have any.

But author name can be tricky. If you're a famous author like Stephen King or Nora Roberts, your name sells your books. And it's the name that matters more than the title or even the cover image.

Sometimes using a larger author name can imply that you're a best-selling author even when you aren't. But I suspect that will change over time as more people try that trick and then readers get savvy to the fact that just because a name on the cover is big it doesn't mean a best-selling or interesting book.

Basically, when determining relative font sizes ask yourself what you want the reader to see first, and make that the largest element, preferably at the top. Although, once more, pay attention to your category or genre because some have very strong trends towards where title and author name are placed.

ALIGNMENT

One final thing to be aware of when dealing with fonts. Each letter in a font is essentially in a small equally-sized rectangle. Different letters will fill that rectangle to different degrees. A lower case letter for example, will not fill that rectangle as much as the same letter in upper case. And the lower-case letter "g" is going to fill that space more than the lower-case letter "e" as another example.

Each word you use is created by combing these rectangles. This becomes an issue when you try to use a program like Affinity to center a line of text. Because Affinity is centering that text based upon the rectangle that contains each letter, not the actual top and bottom of the letters on the page. You can tell Affinity to center that text and it will do so, correctly, using the rectangles, but to the naked eye the text will not be centered.

This is especially an issue with fonts that I think of as "bottom-heavy". These fonts tend to leave more white space above the tops of the letters than below the bottom of the letters.

Which means, depending on the font you choose, you may need to manually center your text in situations like that. (Or choose a better font that doesn't have that issue.)

This is especially important to keep an eye on when looking at the spine of a print book where it becomes very noticeable.

It's also why I often will use all caps on the spine of a book rather than upper- and lower-case letters. That can go a long ways towards alleviating the issue.

Another thing to keep in mind is that some fonts are good at creating ligatures for you and some are not. Due to the nature of certain letters in a font, they can potentially overlap in ugly ways. So "f" and "i" is an example where for some fonts the f curves down enough to almost hit the dot on the i. A good font will swap out the individual letters for a ligature that combines the two in a visually appealing way.

Especially when looking at your title or larger text elements, pay attention to the spacing between individual letters. You may need to manually adjust the space between two letters to make things look "right".

Okay. On to a new topic, series branding.

SERIES BRANDING

If you're creating covers for a related series of books, you want readers to instantly know those books belong together.

This means that you have to make the covers consistent across the collection or series.

A perfect example of this is the J.D. Robb books. She's up to 55 books as I write this and once you get past the first three books, all of the covers share a common appearance. The author name is always in the same place, uses the same font, and takes up about the same amount of space on the cover. Same with title placement and the central cover image.

Here are four of the books in that series:

They clearly belong together.

(This is also a perfect example of what I was talking about with big author names, because the first three books did not have the author name dominating the space, but the covers from book four onward do.)

The design is not perfectly aligned across all of those covers, but they still clearly belong together.

And these covers also show that there's plenty of room for variety even within those constraints by changing up the color of the author name, the background color behind the name, and the image used.

When you set out to create the first cover for a series or related collection of titles, you need to think about the entire series and what you can do to have consistent branding across it so that readers immediately know that this is an X series book. This includes thinking through the different titles you might use and making sure that your design can accommodate them.

Also, I want to add here that it is fine to get inspiration from someone else's covers, but do not under any circumstances copy the overall branding of someone else's cover. That is a trademark violation. Even if they don't have that overall look trademarked they can still sue you because trademark is about brand recognition and the fact that someone mistook your book for theirs means you took it too far.

Your cover should never be designed in such a way that it is mistaken for someone else's books. I've seen this only a handful of times in the last eight years because it's almost impossible to copy so many elements from someone else's cover that you get mistaken for their cover. We're not talking common elements, like glowy hands in urban fantasy. This is top to bottom, same element placement, same font, same colors, etc. Do not be that asshole.

* * *

Okay, those are the basics of design. There's far more to it and I would encourage you to research more because it is so important to selling books, but this is not a book about design principles, this is a book about putting your design elements together to make book covers.

So let's move on and do that.

I'm going to assume your workspace is already organized like mine from the ads creative book, but if it isn't at a minimum make sure that your Layers studio is in the top right corner and your Transform studio is in the bottom right corner.

EBOOK COVER WITH A CENTRAL IMAGE

Okay. Let's start with an easy one, and that's an ebook cover that uses a single image and solid-colored block for the text like we just saw with the J.D. Robb covers.

There can be a lot of variety in taking this approach. Here are two different covers I've designed over the years that use a central image.

 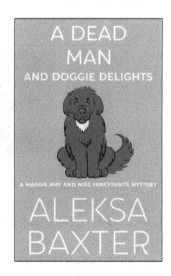

They're great for short story collections or long series that need uniformity across books.

For example, here are the first four books in the Puppy Love series:

They clearly fit together, right? And all I had to do was change out the photo, change the number for the book in the series, and change the title. Everything else stays the same for each story.

Which means that once the template is in place it only takes about five minutes to create each new cover. Maybe ten. The hardest part is finding a good image to use.

That and dealing with any issues if the title for a particular book or story is significantly different and messes up the design. But that's why you try not to have titles that are vastly different across a series.

The other option is to use a layout like I did with the M.H. Lee titles that uses a design that allows for vastly different title lengths but still keeps that uniformity of appearance:

(Those might've taken a little longer than five minutes each because of the font I chose for the cover which required some playing around each time.)

Alright then. For this first cover, we're going to create a new Puppy Love cover from scratch.

I'm going to assume you know how to create a new document and, if wanted, a preset, and that your workspace is set up for working with images. That was all covered in *Affinity Publisher for Ad Creatives*, but see the Appendix for the short version of how to do each if you don't remember or didn't read that book first.

Step one is to start with a new document that fits ebook cover dimensions. Mine are currently set to 1600 x 2560. I used to use 1563 x 2501.

(Don't ask me why I changed. I think the first set of dimensions I used came straight from Amazon's help text somewhere, but the second set made Vellum happier, but don't quote me on that. Both of those dimensions work fine on all retailers as far as I've seen.)

So, File->New, enter the dimensions or use your preset, RGB/8 is fine for the color, and profile for the orientation.

As for DPI…I personally use 300 DPI for any cover I'm creating even ebook, because this lets me bring that ebook cover image into my print layouts without worrying about the image being blurry when printed.

The minimum DPI you want for print is 300 and the only way to effectively get that throughout your design process is to start with it. (We'll discuss the mistakes I've made in this regard more when we talk about creating a print cover.)

The reason not to use 300 DPI for an ebook cover is potential file size. But you can fix some of that with your export settings.

So I'm going with 300 DPI. You should at least use a minimum of 72 DPI.

Once you have your settings, click Create and you will have a nice white space to work with.

Before we do anything else, let's place guide lines to divide our space into thirds. I'm working with 1600 x 2560 so that means 533 and 1066 for my vertical lines and 853 and 1707 for my horizontal lines.

You can place guide lines by left-clicking on the ruler along the left-hand edge or the top of the workspace and then dragging them into place. You will see a small box appear with the position of the guideline as you drag it into place.

Stop when you reach the location you want. Left-click on the line and drag again to adjust if you get it wrong the first time. That will leave you with something like this where the blue lines are my guide lines that are dividing my cover into nine sections.

(To avoid having to do this every single time you create a cover, you may want to save this blank cover with guide lines as its own file that you can start with next time you want to create a cover.)

For the Puppy Love covers, I devoted the top third to the title and series information so our next step is to place a solid fill for the top third and a picture frame for the bottom two-thirds.

To do this, click on the Rectangle Tool on the left-hand side and click and drag in the workspace to create a solid-colored rectangle in the top third of the cover. Then click on the Picture Frame Rectangle Tool on the left-hand side and click and drag to form the picture frame in the bottom two-thirds of the cover.

Remember that you want Snapping Enabled (top menu with the horseshoe shaped magnet, in the dropdown click on the checkbox to Enable Snapping) so that when you drag your elements into place you can see the red and green lines that show that they are aligned with your other elements, the perimeter of the cover, and/or the guide lines you placed.

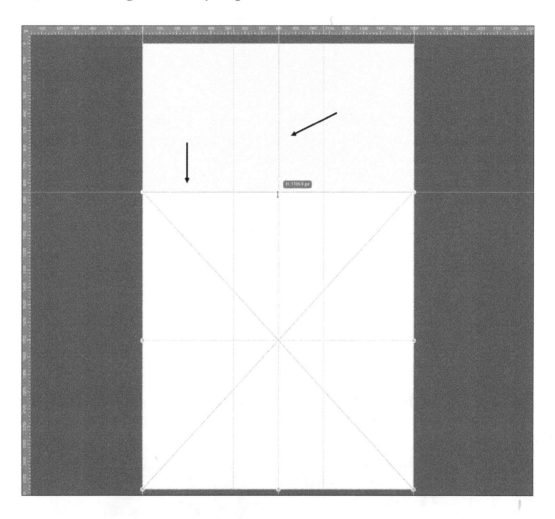

In the image above there is a red line across the canvas at the one-third mark where we placed a guide line and also there's one through the center of the picture frame to show that it's centered in the space. We could click and drag out and then back on any of the perimeter lines to see that the frame is aligned with the edges of the workspace as well. (I already did that as I clicked and dragged to place the frame.)

Next, we want to change the color of the Rectangle we placed, so click on the rectangle layer in the Layers studio:

We now have a few choices for changing the color of the rectangle. We can go to the dynamic menu at the top which has a rounded rectangle next to the word Fill, click on that, and choose a color from there:

Or, we can click on the Color studio, double-click on the solid-filled circle which shows our current color, and then use the Color Chooser to find or specify our color.

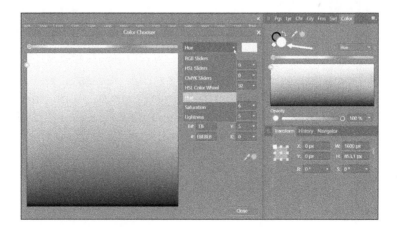

As you can see in the image above, there are a number of different approaches to choose from in the dropdown provided for the Color Chooser.

If I'm just moving between basic colors like black and white or I'm using a color I've already used in my design, I go with the Fill option at the top of the workspace. But if I have a specific color I want to use or want to really experiment with choosing a new color, I use the Color studio.

So let's go with the Color studio right now. I'm going to choose the HSL Color Wheel option. And I want some sort of bright pink.

These are ebook-only covers so I don't need to worry about how the color will print which means I can do something bright and not worry too much about how dark it will be when printed.

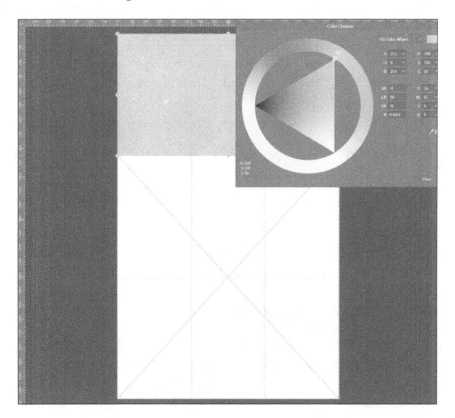

I like that color on my high resolution monitor. It looks nice and bright pink. But interestingly enough—and I can't show you this, unfortunately—when I look at the screenshot of this on my laptop I see a more muted, almost purple color.

And I think this is important to understand. That not all of your viewers are going to experience whatever it is you create in the same way. It will depend very much on the device they are using to view your cover. I've also seen this difference when I move from my PC laptop where I design my covers to my Apple laptop where I generate my Vellum ebook files.

But I know right now, just looking between my laptop and my monitor, that some users are going to see a bright pink background on this cover and others are going to see a more muted purple.

If it's really important to me that everyone see pink, then I need to click further along on the color wheel towards red.

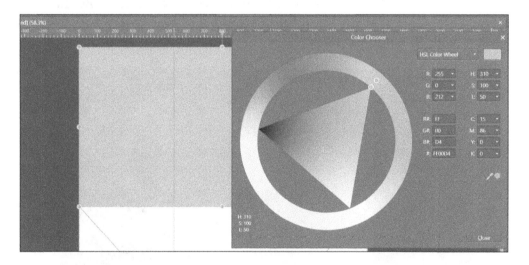

I now have a very vibrant pink on my monitor and a more muted pink on my laptop screen, but at least they're both pink, so we'll go with it.

While I'm here, I may want to write down my HSL values for this color, in this case 310, 100, and 50. Because for the heart I'm going to put on this section to show which number in the series a title is, I want a color that's as vibrant as the one I'm using for the background.

Since my S value is 100 I probably don't need to do this, but when you get away from the color extremes—so the colors in the triangle rather than around the perimeter—it can matter more if you want the colors to feel like they belong together.

By keeping my S at 100 and my L at 50 I can change the H value to get bright blues, greens, yellows, etc. that all feel like they go with my pink.

One more thing to mention before we move on from the color wheel. For a series if you do want to use different colors consider dividing the color wheel into sections and then changing the H value by the same amount for each new cover.

So I might go from 310 for this pink to 250, which gives me a bright blue, to 190 which is a lighter blue, to 120 which is a bright green, to 60 which is a bright yellow. It's possible not all of the colors will be ones you want to use—I'd probably skip the light blue—but doing that can give you a range of colors to play with that also seem to fit together well as opposed to being more random about it.

Okay.

Time to add text. I don't think I did this with the original covers, but I'm going to use a text frame here so that the text stays in the same space even when we change up the title. So let's click on the Frame Text Tool (the T in a gray box) and then draw a frame for our title text.

Ideally you never want to take any of your key image elements to the edge of the cover. It should have a little room to breathe. (I am admittedly bad at remembering this.)

And looking at this space I don't think trying to contain either the series name or the title to one-third of the space we're working with is going to look good, but maybe what I can do is use that golden ratio and make my text frame fit a 1 to 1.6 ratio.

It's not going to be visible to the viewer that I've done that, because my text won't ever fill the entire space, but it might help to block out that space.

So my top text frame is going to be 788 W by 493 H. And then I'm going to draw a second text frame below that that's the same width, but only 110 H. (I may adjust that later.)

Let's put some text in each of those boxes.

I'll start with the author name, in this case "C. Coal". To do so, I make sure I'm clicked onto that layer in my Layers studio, click on the A for the Artistic Text Tool, and then click into that text frame in my workspace and type in the name.

I now have the top left corner of that text frame showing C. Coal in black, Arial, 12 pt because that's the default.

I select all (Ctrl +A) and then click on the black rectangle in the dynamic menu up top and change my color to white. I was able to just double-click on the white full circle in the dropdown but if that wasn't white I could've gone to the Swatches tab and clicked on the white swatch there.

I also changed my font size to 24 pt.

I want left-aligned, so that's fine, but I'm going to go into the alignment dropdown and center that text vertically as well as you can see in the screenshot below.

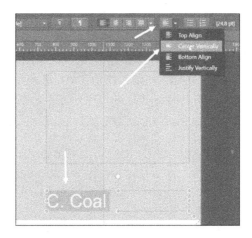

Most designers would probably say that Arial is a boring font you should never use for a cover design. Just like using Times New Roman on a cover. Which, fine, whatever. It doesn't really have a personality so I can see that, but I don't find it objectionable to use it either. If what you want is something that is innocuous and conveys information without interference, I think it works well for that.

But let's go hunting for a better font to use.

To do that, click on the dropdown for the font in the top menu. (Or in the Character studio if you'd rather use that). And you should see a listing of available fonts like this:

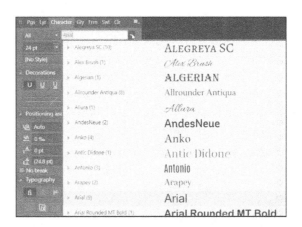

I have a lot of fonts. (DesignCuts and their bundles have been my downfall.)

And because with cover design you need to be careful that you have a commercial license for the font you use, I actually went through one day and created for myself a PDF that shows each of the fonts I have a license to use.

(Because the ones that are there as part of Microsoft Office, for example, are not necessarily available for your commercial use in your cover design even though Affinity might pull them up for you.)

It's an Excel file which means if I know I want a specific type of font, like serif or sans-serif, I can filter the file to just that type of font. But I also have it in PDF so I can scan through visually, too.

I put the word "Handgloves" in front of each of the fonts so I could see how it treated that word, which is supposed to be a good word to use to see how a font handles ascenders and descenders. (That's the d and l and the g.)

Also, I have a personal issue with how some fonts handle a "g", especially script fonts, so writing Handgloves let me see that easily.

Here's the first page of the PDF:

Sample (20 pt)	Style	Font Name
HANDGLOVES ARISTELLE SANS	Display	Handgloves Aristelle Sans
Handgloves Bauhaus 93	Display	Handgloves Bauhaus 93
HANDGLOVES BEACHWOOD SANS	Display	Handgloves Beachwood Sans
Handgloves	Display	Handgloves Betterworks
Handgloves BlackChancery	Display	Handgloves BlackChancery
Handgloves Boyz R Gross	Display	Handgloves Boyz R Gross
Handgloves Bradley Gratis	Display	Handgloves Bradley Gratis
Handgloves Bradley Hand ITC	Display	Handgloves Bradley Hand ITC
Handgloves Brittanic Bold	Display	Handgloves Brittanic Bold
Handgloves Broadway	Display	Handgloves Broadway
HANDGLOVES BRUNCHES	Display	Handgloves Brunches
HANDGLOVES BRUSHABS	Display	Handgloves Brushabs
HANDGLOVES BUSHCRAFT SANS	Display	Handgloves Bushcraft Sans
HANDGLOVES CARENTRO	Display	Handgloves Carentro
Handgloves Carolingua (Bigfoot)	Display	Handgloves Carolingua (Bigfoot)

Ignore the "Handgloves" part of the font name in the third column. That was just my weirdness putting it in there and I've been too lazy to have Excel strip it back out for me.

(Looking at this you can also see how different fonts have vastly different heights at the same point size. Look at Betterworks compared to Beachwood Sans. These are all in 20 pt font.)

For this cover I want something fairly simple and maybe a little fun. Which means Brunches might be a good option for the title and author name.

I have it listed as a display font, but it's also sans-serif which is what I want. (For my listing if I think a font could be main body text for the interior that's what I show as a serif or sans-serif, but if I think it would work on a cover but not in the main body of a document I show it as display even if it is also serif or sans-serif. I like to be confusing, but it works for me.)

So looking at these fonts…

Something like Beachwood Sans or Bauhaus have too much personality for what I want here. The series name portion is going to be in a script font, so I want a font for the title and author name that doesn't fight with that.

I can go back into Affinity and actually try these out in real-time. As I slowly move my mouse over each font in the dropdown menu, Affinity will change my text on the canvas to that font. Like here where it's applied the Brunches font to my author name:

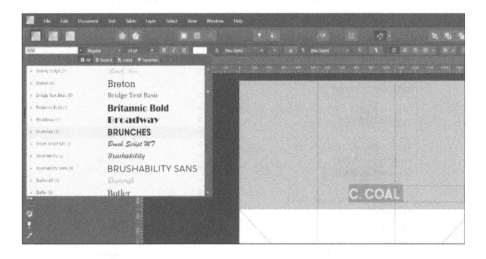

It's just doing this temporarily. I'd have to actually click on the font name for Affinity to permanently apply it to the text. But scrolling down is a quick way to see which fonts may or may not work in the design. (Just always be sure to check that you have the license for the font before you finalize your design.)

If I think a font might work, I'll usually save or export a draft version of the cover with that font applied and then keep looking for other options.

I want to say with the original of this cover I came up with twenty-five different possibilities.

Once I have those possible covers exported to a file I can then go to the folder where I saved them and start doing a side-by-side elimination. I look at Cover 1 and Cover 2 and decide that 1 is better so delete 2. And then that 3 is better than 1 and so delete 1. And so on and so on until I get down to about five covers that are all equally fine

And then I pick one out of the remaining group.

Here I think Brunches was a little chunky for what I wanted. Brushability Sans was a little thin. It turns out in this case that I used a font called Explorer Sans and I used the bold version. This font does come in smaller than other fonts at this point size so I also needed to increase the font size to use it.

A quick note here. I've been talking about fonts but I also tend to use the term font for font family, which is a technical no-no. So let me break that down real quick.

Explorer Sans Regular is a font. Explorer Sans Bold is technically a *different* font because it's a different weight. Both would be considered part of the same font family because they have the same general appearance and design.

Where it gets confusing is that I also have an Explorer P Sans and an Explorer Script option which are probably technically considered part of the Explorer font family, but one has a rough surface appearance and the other is a script font.

So I just in my sloppy way refer to fonts which can either be the individual font, Explorer Sans Bold, or can be the entire family. Keep that in mind for the next little bit.

Okay.

If you don't have various weights/styles of a font, they won't be options for you to choose from in Affinity. Like here, the font I have right above Explorer Sans is called Euphoria Script, but I only have one weight of that font so my dropdown for weight for that font only lists Regular as an option:

I also can't do italics for that font. It is what it is.

Compare that to Kenac where I have ten options available, five different weights, all with an italic ("It") version:

With this one I can keep the appearance of the Kenac font, but have various versions of it on my cover that are thinner or thicker or slanted.

Always keep that in mind when selecting the fonts you're going to use on your cover.

If you're going to have a lot of text elements like title, author name, series name, and review quote, for example, you may want to choose a font family that has multiple weights and italic versions to give you some variety in your design.

What you do not want to do is use more than two font families—including any display fonts—in your design. And only use one serif font family and one sans serif font family at a time. Do not have your two font families be two serif families or two sans serif families.

Each font family you choose needs to be different enough to hold its own.

Okays. So Explorer Sans. And I'm going to make it 36 pt.

This brings up an interesting issue I mentioned to you before, and that's fonts that are bottom-heavy or that basically don't fit evenly in their text frame. Because look at this:

I have that text centered vertically. It should be sitting in the center of the text frame with equal amounts of space above and below the letters. But it is not. And if I align it to the top it doesn't go to the top. Align it to the bottom and it's fine, but there's extra space built in above the letters of this font.

So if I were to use this right now and have Affinity center that text top to bottom on my page the text would not in fact be centered. The space the text is in would, but not the actual letters, which is what really matters.

So be careful when choosing your font that you pay attention to something like this and realize the issues it's going to cause you. Here it doesn't cause me any issue, but if I were to do a print version of this cover and use the same font on the spine, it definitely would.

Okay.

Let me add a title for this one into the text frame above. I'm going to call this one Spring Fling. So I click on the A for the Artistic Text Tool, click into the other text frame, and type in my text. And then I have to change my font, font size, color, and weight.

Looking at it, I think that I actually want the font size to go up to 48 instead of 36, so now I do that for both text frames.

But we run into an issue. The text frame I have for the author name isn't large enough to display 48 pt text in this font. Affinity indicates that by not displaying the text on my canvas, but instead showing red circles along the perimeter of the text frame. There's also an alert in the Preflight studio.

I can still see the text in the Layers studio however.

I have two choices. Change the font size back or change the size of the text frame.

I am going to change the size of the text frame. To do so I click on the frame in the Layers studio, click on the blue circle at the top of the frame in my workspace, and drag until my text becomes visible again. Since the text frame for my author name and for my title still don't overlap, that's all I have to do.

But we have another issue to deal with now. I don't like the spacing between the lines in my title section:

I think those lines are too far apart.

There are two choices you have here to fix this.

You can use separate text frames for each line of text and manually space them until you get an appearance you like. This is often the answer when you have words like "the" and "to" that are small and you have to include them because they're part of the title, but don't want them to be as large as the rest of your text.

Or you can leave the text together and go to the Character studio and change the line spacing, otherwise known as Leading.

To do that, select your text and then go to the Character studio and click on the dropdown arrow for leading override. Hold your mouse over each option to see what it will look like on the canvas until you get one that works.

In this case I decided that 30 is a little too tight and 36 is a little too loose, so I typed in 32. That works for me.

(And another note here that design is subjective. There are probably some who'd feel those letters are crowding each other a little too much and would go with the 36 pt setting. And maybe tomorrow I would, too. That's why it's good to try to let a design sit a bit if you can so you can come back to it after a few days and think, "Yeah, no, that doesn't work" or "Okay, yeah, we're good." Especially as a novice designer. Professionals have things they know work from hundreds of hours of experience. As a novice you have to build that experience. Until you do, expect to make mistakes.)

Okay. Our title and our author name are there. Let's do the easy part and throw in a picture of a cute puppy. So click on the Layers studio, click on the Picture Frame layer, go to the tools on the left-hand side, click on the Place Image Tool, find your image, and open it.

How about a cute bulldog:

That's how the image came in. He's actually pretty well positioned according to the guide lines, but I think I want to make him a little bigger. I also don't like the pink of the flowers behind him compared to the pink in the background up top. That background pink is back to looking to purple for me.

Since this is a series cover, assuming it wasn't the first one, I wouldn't be able to change that background color. So if that clash were enough of a problem for me I'd have to choose a different image because I'm not advanced enough (or interested enough) in changing the color of the flowers in the image.

But since this is the first cover we've done for this series, we can change that background color.

First, I'm going to increase the size of the image and reposition it. I can either use the slider below the image to change its size and click in the center of the four arrows on the image to reposition it, or I can click on the picture frame layer, click down to the image, and resize and move from there.

Now for the color. I go to the Color studio and use the eyedropper tool to grab a pink from the flowers behind the dog. Remember, left-click on the eyedropper and hold as you hover over the canvas. Let up when you find a color you like. Double-click on the circle next to the eyedropper to actually apply it:

Much better.

That's actually much more pink than the background on the cover was before. Also, increasing the size of the image and bringing that dog into the center rectangle in our rule of thirds really makes his cute little face the focus.

Which is good, because this series of stories is basically for people who love puppies and want to read about them bringing two people together for a stress-free happily ever after. The dog is what is meant to sell the story.

Okay. Now we need to add the series name on the left-hand side and the series number. Since this one isn't going to be changed from cover to cover we can type the text directly onto our cover. So I click on the Artistic Text tool, click on my cover, and type in Puppy, enter, Love.

You'll notice as you work with fonts that sometimes the spacing between lines will be different depending on whether the text wraps to the next line or you use an enter to get text to the next line. All I'd say for that is to choose one or the other to keep it consistent.

Or, as I mentioned above, separate each line of text into its own layer.

Once more we need to change the color, size, font, and line spacing.

Since I used Explorer Sans for the title and author name I'm going to use Explorer Script for the series name. The two fonts are meant to work together and if you have font combinations like that it can sometimes be a good way to have that variety of fonts on your cover but also know that they are made to be paired with one another.

Now it's time to angle our text. There are two options here. You can left-click on the white circle above the text box and drag until the text is at an angle you like.

Or you can enter a new R value in the Transform studio. For the original covers I used 15 degrees, but I like 20 degrees better this time around.

Once I have the angle set and the size set I can drag that text into place. I added an extra guide line so that I could align the top of the Puppy text with the top of the title. I also adjusted the font size so that the bottom of my series name lines up with the bottom of the rectangle I created for the title text to fit in.

We'll see if we keep it that way, but here it is:

Now all we need is the heart with the number on it to tell us which book this is in the series.

To add a heart shape, go to the Rectangle Tool, click on the white dropdown arrow, and choose the Heart Tool. Then click and drag a heart on the cover just like you would a rectangle.

First things first, let us change the color of that heart.

I want to do this in the Color studio, so go there, and double-click on the pink that's the current color to bring up the Color Chooser dialogue box. Mine is still on the HSL Color Wheel screen since that's what I used last.

(My S and L values are different from what I wrote down above because we changed our pink.)

I want blue but I'm going to keep S as 91 and L as 56. I can just click over along the perimeter of the wheel to get that. And, perfect.

But I want my heart angled like my series title, so I'm going to change that R value to a 20 in the Transform studio.

Note that the Transform studio (and other bottom-level studios) can move around a bit dependent upon which top-level studio you have open. I tend to think it's disappeared on me when it's really just moved up to the midpoint because I have a studio open that doesn't require as much space and have no studios anchored in the middle.

Okay. I can now drag the blue heart into position and adjust its size until I like how it fits with the other elements. In this case I do so until it lines up with the bottom of the word Love and also along the first-third dividing line.

Now I need to add a number on top of that. Click away from the heart, click on A for Artistic Text Tool, click back on the canvas, add the number, change the font, color, etc., change the angle, resize. Click on the Move Tool black arrow and then click and drag the number on top of the heart.

If the number disappears when you do this (as it just did to me) then the number layer is below the heart layer in the Layers studio, and you need to go to the Layers studio and click and drag it up.

If it's still not positioned perfectly, you can use the up and down and right and left arrows to adjust its position on the canvas.

If you decide you want to resize the heart at this point, I'd recommend grouping the heart and number layers so you can resize them together. (Select both and use Ctrl + G to group them.)

Here's the result:

If this was a new cover design I might tweak this a bit more (there's a lot of space there between the title and the author name and I think I'd move the heart around a bit more), but overall I think it does what it needs to do, which is draws the eye to a cute puppy and implies that it's a sweet romance.

You can use this basic design for other genres, though. Just for kicks, let me change this up a smidge to show you.

An image, series name, and some color changes and here we have a sexy romance instead of a clean and sweet one:

That took about five minutes for me, if that. Granted, the colors here are more for a fun summer fling series than say, a broody bad boy series. But you get the idea that you can use a template like this and then change up the feel of the cover with the image you choose, the font you use, and the colors.

Both of these rely heavily on the image to bring in the reader. One says, "cute puppies." The other says, "hot dude taking off his shirt." For their respective audiences, that draws the eye.

Okay. Now let's take a quick look at an ebook cover that uses a side image instead and leaves two-thirds of the space for the title information. This one we're going to put a lot more attention on font elements because that's what dominates the space.

EBOOK COVER WITH A SIDE IMAGE

Now we're going to build another basic ebook cover that uses a single image and a solid-colored background for the text, but this time the image will be just one-third of the cover and most of the focus is going to be on the title information.

First we need our ebook cover. I saved a version of a blank ebook cover with guide lines on it, so to open that I go to File->Open Recent and choose that file from the dropdown menu. If it wasn't one I'd used recently, I'd do File->Open and navigate to where I had it saved.

This one we're going to put the image for each cover on the left-hand third of the canvas. I'd say this is very much a short story or non-fiction style.

So, Picture Frame Rectangle tool, click and drag to fill the left-hand third of the cover space from top to bottom using the green and red alignment lines to make sure we've hit the edge.

Keep in mind that sometimes it's easier to click and drag onto the canvas and then move each line around the perimeter into position along the edges.

Next, Rectangle Tool. In my case, because the last time I used the "shape tool" it was a heart, I'm currently seeing a blue heart in my left-hand set of icons. But I can click on that white arrow next to the heart, choose the Rectangle Tool, and draw my rectangle in the other two-thirds of the cover.

Mine came in as light gray, so I click on the Fill box in the dynamic menu up top and I turn it black using the Swatches tab:

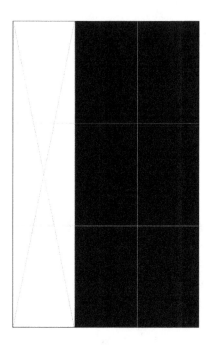

Very boring. But let's add our image.

Click on the Picture Frame layer in the Layers studio and then use the Place Image Tool to find an image to place on that left-hand third.

I used this design for my speculative fiction covers which are often "an interesting but abstract idea" so that's what I'm going to use for the cover image. Basically I just want something that's different for each one and, honestly with these, I expect the collection to sell not the individual short stories. The individual short stories exist more for me to offer one up for free to drive interest to the collection.

I will also say with both the prior short story series and this one, I don't see many sales of either one. The only short story series I've ever seen good sales on were billionaire romance or erotica. But maybe you will do better. Or you can use a short story as a lead magnet into your series. (Although, as a novel reader the short stories my authors write tend not to do much for me, but that's probably just me.)

Anyway. I'm getting away from what we're doing. So, let's add the image.

But first, let me just take a moment here to talk about stock photos. My advice to you is going to be (a) pay for them and (b) make sure you read the license for the photos you use.

I get my photos from Shutterstock, Depositphotos, and DesignCuts. All of those allow me to use their images in book covers. There was some other site that had an AppSumo deal a few years back where I had to cancel the deal because when I read the terms it didn't seem like I'd be able to use those images the way I needed to.

Also, at least when I first started using them, I noticed that Depositphotos had a time cap on downloaded images. I was buying monthly download packs at the time and it basically said I had to use those downloaded photos within X days. Shutterstock did not.

I now buy the AppSumo Depositphotos deal when it's offered each year around November and that gives me download credits I can then use when I need an image, so that I'm always within that use period.

Can you stretch things? Sure, probably. Do you want to take that risk? Eh…It can be expensive if you get caught out. So always know where you got an image from and what the rights you have to use it are.

The reason I avoid the free sites is because there have been times someone loaded images to one of those sites that were not theirs and then you can get sued for a nice chunk of change if you use that image.

Also, it should be obvious, but just because an image is on the internet does not make it available for you to use. It is copyrighted just like everything you write is copyrighted. So if you don't want people stealing your shit, don't steal theirs.

Okay then. We now have a cover that has an image on the left-hand side and a black space to work in on the right two-thirds of the cover.

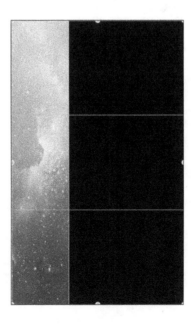

Time to put in our text. I'm going to use one of my obnoxiously-long titles so we have a lot to work with: By Your Side When the Sun Sets by M.H. Lee.

(The real cover for this one has a dragon image in that left-hand third, but right now I'm just using a galaxy background.)

I'm going to use a font I purchased, Desire, for the title and author name because I want you to see how to use the Glyph Browser.

The first thing we need to do before we type in our text is ask, how are we going to split that up? It's messy, right? Where's the emphasis in that title? On Your? Or By? Or Side? Or Sun Sets?

We don't have to stick to this; we can change our minds later. But for now…

I think I'll split it into thirds with "By Your Side", "When", and "the Sun Sets" as my three lines of text. But I'm going to put "the" and "Sun Sets" as separate layers because I want to keep "the" small.

So let's do that.

Choose the Artistic Text Tool and create layers for each of those.

Because it's a black background I need to change the text to white so I can see it. I'm also going to change my font over before I start typing since I have four layers to create and that means less work for me.

You don't have to worry about size right now, but you can.

With the Artistic Text Tool you can actually left-click and drag to form an A (that is not going to be there once you start to type) if you're not sure what font size you need. Just drag to about the desired height for your letters and then type.

Another thing you can do is get all four layers entered and then select all of the layers in the Layers studio. That will put a box around all four of them that you can then click and drag from the corner to change the size of them all at once.

So I input my text and here we are:

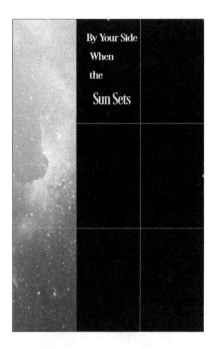

Obviously we're not going to leave it this way. That does not look good. But the first step is always getting the components in place.

Now we need to make some decisions. The first one is where we want to place the title.

I'm thinking the top third. If we place it in the middle third that leaves a lot of dead space up top that won't get used. But if we put the title in the top third of the cover that will leave the middle for any subtitle information and the bottom for the author name.

I'd only put author name at the top if it was a recognizable name that could sell the book on name alone like Stephen King or Nora Roberts. But for us mere mortals, better to put title up top, author down below.

Okay, so that's decided.

Next we get to play around with how to arrange these words. And, really, that comes down to genre and personal preference and design skill. (I can bet money at least one person reading this book can arrange these words better than I'm about to. And to that person I apologize for the painful experience of watching me get it wrong.)

Word placement also depends a lot on the font you're using and the actual words in the title.

Let me show you what I mean. The first word in this title is "By" which means we can maybe do something interesting with that capital B.

Let's go to the Glyph Browser studio and see what our options are:

Not bad. I have fifteen variants on a capital B to choose from in this font. (But not the twenty-seven I'd have for a capital A)

What about an S or a T. Let's look at that next:

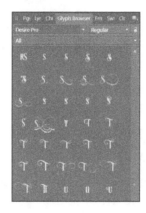

A decent number of choices. W has about the same.

I also have lower-case letters to potentially play with. And, again, some letters will have more choices than others.

And keep in mind that most fonts will not have this much variety. My first YA fantasy covers used a font called Jupiter which has a couple of alternates for letters like R—there are two fancy ones to choose here—but not near the insane variety that Desire does.

And it also has some ligatures, like these:

So there are some choices that can be made to spice up the text design, but it very much depends on the font and it depends on the letters in the words in the title.

I show you all of this because when I was first looking at covers and thinking, "Wow, that's fancy" I assumed that the cover designer had added all of the flourishes or extensions to the title themselves.

I thought all those whirls and swirls were part of the design work they did. But the reality is that in a lot of instances they just know the right font to use and how to choose the alternates.

Now, neither one of the fonts I just showed you is free. I bought Jupiter because I wanted to be able to match the font used on the covers for my YA fantasy series. And I bought Desire, because, wow, look at all those choices.

(I only learned about Desire, though, after someone I know who is good at covers looked at a mockup a designer had done for a cover for me and said, "Oh,

I think that's using that Desire font that everyone seems to be using these days." So be careful jumping on that particular bandwagon.)

Anyway. Back to our cover and our text.

There are an infinite number of options for how to combine the seven words in this title. And it's very easy to take a font like Desire and get out of control with it. Allow me to demonstrate:

This is just too much. In thumbnail all you see are a bunch of swirls everywhere. Kudos to the font that it doesn't look even worse, but it's bad. People can and do have different aesthetics—I mean some people like toilets made of gold, right—but I'm willing to go out on a limb here and assume that at least nine out of ten people would find this overdone.

So flourishes are nice, but not on every single letter. And certainly not for mainstream science fiction and fantasy.

Okay. Let's do a quick review on how to apply one of these and then we'll try some more reasonable designs.

If the letter is already in the workspace (like here) and you want to replace it, highlight the letter, then go to the Glyph Browser studio, pull up your font, find the version you want to use to replace that letter, and double-click on it.

Remember that you can start to type in the font name in the top menu to find the font and its options faster. Or just scroll through the dropdown menu until you find the font you want.

If there is no letter to replace, just click into your workspace where you want to insert the letter and then go to the Glyph Browser studio and double-click on the option you want.

Recently-used glyphs will be at the bottom of the studio so that you can just double-click on them from there instead of having to look them up.

So let's see what we can do with this text.

First things first, I'm going to move "the" so that it's on the same line with

"Sun Sets". If you have snapping enabled (which you should), you can see when two layers are aligned as you drag them together. Like here where the red line indicates that they're aligned along the bottom of the two text layers:

I can also align vertically. In that case, it's a green line that shows.

I'm going to see what happens when I align the "By", "When" and "the" on the left-hand side.

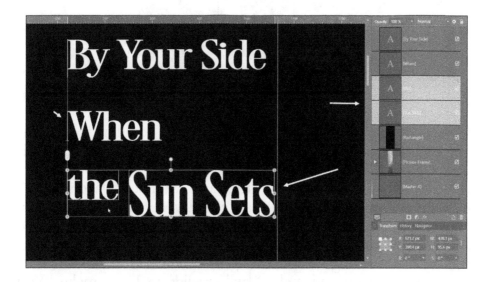

If you want to move two text layers at once, select both of their layers first in the Layers studio by clicking on one and then holding down the Ctrl key or Shift key to select the other. Ctrl if they're not adjacent, Shift or Ctrl if they are.

I've zoomed in here (View->Zoom and then pick an option, I chose 200%) to make it easier to see my text. Usually I don't do this because I like to also see how the elements I'm working on fit in the overall design. (And you'll see in a minute that this created a problem for me.)

Now it's time to make this interesting in some way.

We could just align the text and change some font sizes around and leave it plain. Here I've taken the size of "Sun Sets" which is 32.8 pt and divided that by 1.6 to get 20.5 pt for "the" and then applied those two font sizes to "By Your Side" and "When".

I wanted to keep the three lines of text evenly spaced. I could have done it manually by selecting each line and moving it up and down and watching the numbers that appear between the layers until they matched.

But what I did instead is group the "the" and "Sun Sets" layers into one layer and then group all three text lines into another layer. I then selected those three layers and went to the Alignment option up top and chose the Space Vertically option under the Align Vertically section.

This option isn't working for me, though. "When" is too prominent.

So let's change that up and make "By" smaller so I can make "Your Side" bigger to better match the "When".

I'm also going to put "When" and "the" on the same line. That means ungrouping "the" from "Sun Sets" and regrouping it with "When" which I'm also going to put in lower case to further de-emphasize it.

I'm going to center them, too. When I do that, I can see a green line through them like so:

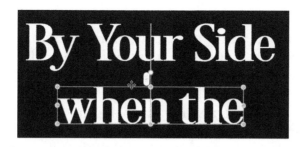

You can also see on that screenshot the distance between the two layers.

After some playing around with font sizes and alternates for the capital letters, here's my new layout.

But I'm still not sold on it. You can see I used special versions for the "B", the "Y" and the "S" in sets. I tried to go with less ornate ones because this isn't that type of story.

But I think the last line is still dominating the space too much.

Here's another option to change the focus some:

I like that better. But that many words on just two lines isn't going to work with our overall design. There's going to be way too much empty space when I zoom out and look at the entire cover. So even though this would work for a more normal cover where the text stretches across the entire width of the cover, it won't work here.

(Also, I noticed when I was working on this example that somehow the "By Your Side" and "Sun Sets portion were looking different even at the same font size, so I deleted Sun Sets, copied By Your Side and replaced the text with Sun Sets so they'd match up. I assume that was from resizing the font by clicking and dragging from the corner. Something to always be on the watch for.)

I'm not done yet, but right now I want to add my author name at the bottom of the cover so I can better see the whole layout.

I can't make it too large because it would pull the eye away from the title, so I think I should center it instead of left-align it.

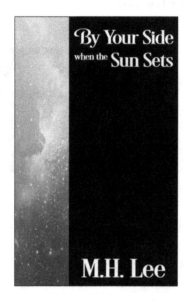

See how there's just a lot of black space there between the title and the author name? I think it's too much.

And, honestly, coming back to this two weeks later after having to evacuate for a large wildfire, it's just kind of boring, isn't it? Like, eh, why would I download this?

(This is why it's always good to let things sit for a bit if you can before you publish them. I am definitely guilty of not doing that most times. I just get a wild hair to change a cover and put something together in a day and throw it up there. But if you can let things sit, you should. And if you can't, you should try to revisit them a month or so later.)

If that doesn't work, what other approach could we take to this?

This is what I originally came up with for this short story:

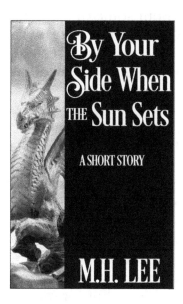

It certainly fills the space better, but that B is a bit too much and I really don't think the "the" needs to be so ornate and I'm kind of hating the alignment of the different text elements on the cover. I think I tried to left-align things and it just didn't work. And what is going on there with Short Story?

(I tell you, I fail in public more times than I can count…)

Here's another attempt:

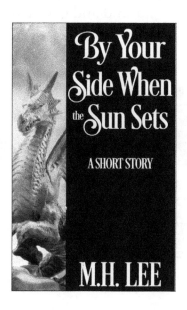

Better. I basically swapped out some of the first letters for different versions in Desire, centered the three lines of text instead of aligning them to the left, and made sure the vertical spacing between each section was the same. I also changed the "the" to a lower case, non-fancy version, and fixed whatever was going on with the short story line.

But I still don't like it.

Honestly, that title is shit. Don't do that to your cover designer. The more you can avoid little filler words like "by", "the", "of", etc. the better in my opinion. Unless it's a literary title.

So I'm going to poke at this a bit more. Maybe see if I can minimize that "by".

When I'm doing something like this, I drop each version I create into a folder and keep going. I will do this with different arrangements of the text, different fonts, different images, etc. and then at the end go look at all of the ideas I came up with side-by-side and pick the winners.

A trained designer would probably be able to do this instinctively without having to go through all the options, but for me it really helps to just try a lot of different approaches and then come back to them when I'm done. Usually what happens is that I end up with the third to last design or so out of twenty or thirty. The first few are crap, I start to narrow in on something that will work, but then I take it a little too far and have to backtrack.

Because the Affinity file thumbnails usually have a preview of the image on them, I always move the .jpg versions into their own folder called something like "images". Then as I compare them I rename them with a 1, 2, 3 etc. in front of the name to shuffle the images around and get them next to each other.

Like this:

I think that first one there is a winner.

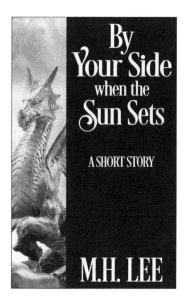

Or good enough for my purposes at least. And good enough for me to go swap that out for the existing one that's up there now.

That's the beauty of self-publishing, it's never too late to try something new and change things up.

(And because I use Vellum to do my own ebook interiors and this title is only out in ebook it takes maybe five minutes to update the ebook file and then the fifteen minutes or so to reload the new file on all the platforms.)

Okay, so we're done with that one for now. Next let's try a cover that uses a single image for the entire cover.

EBOOK COVER WITH A SINGLE IMAGE FOR THE ENTIRE COVER

Alright. Now it's time to create a cover where the entire cover is an image with text overlaid. Because this is basic cover design using Affinity Publisher there are certain tricks that I can't show you.

For example, you can use layer masks in Affinity Photo to blur out the background behind your text and make it more legible when you have a busy background. But that's in Photo not Publisher, so we can't do that.

Which means we have to be very smart about the image we choose for our cover or we need to use cheats like a band across a section of the cover.

First step is to find a good cover image. Many of the images on stock photo sites are good images when they're just sitting there on the screen, but they don't make for good cover images.

Remember when choosing an image that will fill the entire cover that you are working with a rectangular space, so one that's a portrait orientation is going to be better than one that's a landscape orientation. Also, if the entire image is busy, that's going to distract from your text.

Okay.

Let's go look at some examples. We're going to re-do that puppy cover from above, but with a full-cover image.

I'm going to use my Shutterstock images folder for this because the license on those images is one that lets me use them whenever whereas for Depositphotos I try to download images only as I use them due to the wording of their license terms.

This is what we have to choose from:

We have nine stock images here of puppies. The three in the top row as well as the one in the middle would be great choices for the design we used before. They all have bright colors and are landscape orientation so if we pop them into that design they're going to fit well and have an emphasis on the cute puppy.

But they're not ideal as-is for the type of cover we're going to do here because they don't have a lot of space above and below the puppy to place text. Also, especially with the images with grass in the background it's not easy to add on in a way that matches up with the details around the puppies.

The center one we could maybe pull off (and actually will later) because of the blue below, but it's still going to be tricky because it's not a solid blue.

The puppy in the second row on the left has the image orientation that will work and we can possibly fit some text in there at the bottom, but it would probably work better with more advanced design skills. In a situation like this I'd probably tend more towards one of the images with a white background even though that may have less "sophistication" to it.

If I'm not sure what will work, what I like to do is on the stock photo website right-click and save a copy of the images I'm considering to my desktop. I can then put them into my design and see which ones will actually fit the design before I go ahead and purchase the image I want. Yes, the image will be blurry because it's a thumbnail and there will likely be a watermark across it, but it at least lets me get a feel for whether that image has any chance of working.

Right now, though, I'm going to actually use one you don't see here which has two cute puppies in a flower pot and lots of nice white space above. It also uses a bright pink color, so less work for me. (You'll see it in just a minute, don't worry.)

Now that we have an image to work with, let's open Affinity Publisher and start a new book cover. I'm going to start from scratch with this one, no existing guide lines.

My next step is to place the image. I want this in a picture frame so that I can see the boundaries of what will show on my cover. So I start with the Picture Frame Rectangle Tool and use it to draw a rectangle that fits the entire dimensions of my cover.

After that I can go to the Place Image Tool on the left-hand side, navigate to the image I want to use, and select it. Since I'm using a picture frame it will try to fill that space as best as possible. Like this:

That's fine. But I think I actually want that image to be a little larger and repositioned some.

To do that, I can either expand the picture frame layer in the Layers studio to get to the underlying image, click on that image layer, and then go back to my workspace and make my adjustments.

Or I can use the slider below the picture frame to change the image size and click in the center of the four arrows in the center of the image to move it around that way. (Just be careful not to move the picture frame if you use that option. Ctrl + Z is your friend if you do.)

Better. But we have an issue, which is that we're working with an image that has a white background. It looks fine now, but it is going to be a problem when the image is displayed on Amazon and other ebook websites. The cover image will blend into the background so that it's not a distinct thumbnail. (Kind of like what happened with the cover thumbnail we used for the A+ content in the ad creative book where that fact was to our advantage.)

The solution to this is to place a very small light gray border around the cover. And good news. Because we used a picture frame, this should be relatively easy to do. If you don't use a picture frame then you basically need to make your image go not quite to the edge of the document and then you need to put a light gray rectangle layer behind it.

We have a picture frame, though, so let's go ahead and add our border real quick.

Click on the picture frame layer and then go to the dynamic menu up top where it shows Stroke and a line with a red slash next to it that says None.

Click on that line to bring up a border dropdown menu. Change the Width setting to something like .5. It doesn't have to be obvious, it just has to be enough to distinguish your cover from a white background.

The default right now is that the line will be black, but you can also click on that black color box next to Stroke in the dynamic menu and change it using the Swatches tab to a medium gray or even a light gray. Just something that isn't white.

Okay. So now we have an image with a border. Next we need text.

This is when you need to decide if this is a cover for a title that's part of a series or if it's a standalone. Because if it's standalone you can do whatever you want. Obviously, if you have an author brand you'll want to use some of that branding to keep consistency across your titles, even standalones, but you don't have to worry about placing the title and the author name in the same place each and every time.

For a series it really is a good idea to keep that consistent.

Go look at a bunch of authors on Amazon if you don't believe me. See which ones look the best to you in the series thumbnail listings they provide. I would bet you that consistent placement of author name and title really helps keep things looking like they belong together.

And I will tell you it's harder to get that consistency with stock images and using a full-cover image. The reason this series has the covers it does and not covers like the one we're about to create is because it was too hard to get good puppy images that would work well across thirteen covers and let me place my title and author name in the same place each time.

I actually started out with covers like this one and rebranded.

But let's pretend I have a bunch of images that will work. Or that I'm going to be able to pull off one of the other tricks people sometimes can do for a long series, which is that I'm going to stick with this exact image but will change out the pink color for other colors as I go forward. So the next one might be bright blue. The one after that a green. Then orange, etc.

This is a no-name author that readers will not recognize, so let's put the author name in the bottom right corner in a small font size.

I'm going to place this text directly on the workspace, so I use the Artistic Text Tool, click and drag an A in the bottom right corner and then type in the author name, "C. Coal".

It comes out as black, Arial, 25 pt. I want to change that to white and I'm going to use Fontin SmallCaps for my font. So, Ctrl + A to select all and then I can make my changes up top.

Once I do that I adjust the font size and move the text around until I'm happy with it.

Ideally I'd probably want my text a little larger than it is, but I'm dealing with a black line on the image that I don't want to overlap. And since this is Publisher not Photo I don't have good tools for erasing that black line.

I'm going to try a simple layout with Puppy Love in Fontin SmallCaps and then Spring Fling in some sort of scrawled cursive. So I add Puppy Love as one layer and Spring and Fling as their own layers.

I then want Spring and Fling to be in a pink that matches the container the dogs are in, so I use the eyedropper option to grab that color.

At this point I'll go through all of my fonts looking for something that works for that cursive, hate every single one I have for being too lightweight or having a weird p I can't stand, or just otherwise not working, despair that I should've handed this over to a professional but know that would've cost more than the short story will ever make, and then finally settle on something that's okay.

Depending on the day and my mood I may save down about a dozen versions of the cover to compare them side-by-side.

In this case I ended up going with a font called Black Pillow that I didn't find too obnoxious and that at least gives that playful flair to the cover that matches the stories.

I used the rotate option to angle the word "Spring" and then changed the R value in the Transform studio for "Fling" to the same value to make sure that both layers were rotated at the same angle.

And here we go:

I had to move the image around a bit and it now bumps up against my author name in the bottom corner more than I'd like, but I put my guide lines on there to check and I like where they fall for the puppies, so it is what it is.

I think if I had to use this for a series I could do so without a lot of issues. It would probably work best if I kept the same image and swapped out the colors, although doing that successfully would be more of an intermediate-level design skill.

But let's see if I can just swap out the image here using the Document->Resource Manager option.

Let me go bring in another puppy image that has a white background, change the color for the author name text in the bottom, and done:

It works.

If I were designing this series of covers this way from scratch I'd probably drop the puppies in the flower pot and go more with images like this simply because it would give me better consistency across the entire series. I like the puppies in the flower pot more, but there just aren't enough images like them that I could successfully use.

So cover design is kind of like playing pool or chess, you need to be thinking a few moves ahead if you don't want to end up rebranding your covers later.

Alright. So that worked, but let's go back and do a different option.

We're going to choose an image that has no white space in it. But that means image choice becomes even more important.

Here I've brought in that cute chaos puppy with all the background detail.

See how our text has disappeared into the detail? Sometimes if the detail isn't too extreme you can fix this with a contrasting color. But here I don't think that will work, so we'd need color blocks to place our text on.

A lot of times I'll just do a solid line across the bottom or the middle for this. Because, again, we're talking about basic covers here.

But I want to try something different on this one. I want to try to create angled shapes below the pup's face that I can then place my text on.

First things first, insert a small rectangle using the Rectangle Tool.

Theoretically you can then shear the rectangle by clicking near the sides and dragging, but I wasn't able to get that to work. So I went for alternative two, which is to use the Transform studio and change the S value.

Here is a rectangle with an S value of -40 degrees:

That turns out to be too much to go with the text we want to use, so I ended up dialing it back to -25 degrees when I saw the text on it. Which conveniently matches the angle I already had for the text.

It took me some experimenting back and forth to get the rectangle the right size because the "g" in each word takes up a lot of height.

Also, this seems to work best when each word is on its own rectangle and each one has a different background color. Remember, the background color of a rectangle can be changed using the Fill section in the dynamic menu at the top.

When I changed the rectangle color I also had to change the text color for one of my words to white.

And I decided I liked the shapes better when they overlap instead of being separate.

As a final step, I dragged the text layers onto the rectangle layers in the Layers studio so that they were sub-layers of each rectangle.

I then grouped the two rectangles together and used the Align Center option to center the group.

We're just looking at the Spring Fling portion here. I like how the sheared rectangles turned out with the text. I'm not sure I like the image I used because it doesn't go with the colors we've been using for this "brand".

If this was a standalone cover, I might just change the colors. If this was a series, I'd probably choose another image.

So let's do that now. Let's swap out our image for something brighter and cleaner:

Much better.

I still need to fix the author name and series name, though.

Author name I can just make white. Series name I'm going to change to Black Pillow to match the title text and then put on one line and make white.

But that still leaves me the issue of the image. At the size I want it, the image doesn't go to the bottom of the page. See the white space down there?

One possible trick for fixing this is to duplicate that image layer, so right-click in the Layers studio and choose Duplicate, and then flip it and line it up with the original.

To flip an image, go to Layer->Transform->Flip Vertical. Once you do that you can click and drag the image down until the two edges line up.

I also want to Align Horizontally using the options up top and then Group the two and reposition my dog in the center of the cover once more.

When I grouped the two images the X from the picture frame reappeared on top of them. To get rid of it—because it would have been visible in the final product—I had to ungroup them after I'd moved them to their final location.

And here's the final:

If we had put the title text straight on the image it would've probably been a little lost, but by putting those sheared rectangles behind the text we were able to make the text stand out.

Also, it's not ideal to have to duplicate and flip an image layer like we did here. Someone looking really close would probably be able to see the line where that happened, but for an ebook thumbnail cover it should be just fine.

And sometimes, depending on what's at the edge of an image, that won't work. But often with an image where things are subtly changing from light to dark like we have here that's a quick and dirty way to line things up so that the transition is more subtle than trying to use a solid color or trying to copy and cut a section and paste it onto the bottom.

I just want to emphasize one last time that the key with using a full image is making sure that the image you choose works well for a book cover. And if it's for a series you have to remember that it gets much trickier to use full images because every image you choose has to work with all of the series design elements, including placement and colors if you go that direction.

But the nice thing about using a full image like this is it can give depth to your cover that you won't have otherwise. Here we have water drops on a blue surface and the hint of a background behind the dog whereas the cover we did earlier that had white space to work with really didn't have that depth.

As with all covers, though, remember that you're ultimately trying to sell a product. So at the end of the day the question is, does this work for selling this book to the right kind of reader? If the answer is no, then it's the wrong cover no matter how beautiful it is.

Okay. On to print covers.

KDP PAPERBACK COVER

Now let's walk through how to take an existing ebook cover and turn it into a paperback cover using a solid background.

So, again, this is not the fancy, high-end "wow" sort of print cover where the image wraps around the entire cover, but more the basic, functional, gets the job done type.

One of the mistakes I made early on with print covers and still do to some extent, is that I failed to appreciate the variance in the print-on-demand process.

What do I mean by this? I mean that I would put a border around a cover, like this:

And I would fail to realize that sometimes that blue border on the right-hand side was going to be only an eighth of an inch and sometimes it was going to be a quarter of an inch and it could fall anywhere in between. Which meant that sometimes that cover looks lopsided when it prints.

Now, this book has sold a lot of copies with that cover and has decent reviews, so most readers don't seem too freaked out about it, but it annoys me.

Which is why you'll notice that the ebook covers I showed you in this book don't follow that layout. The images we used either cover the entire space, the left-hand side of the space, or the entire cover from left-to-right. That's how I now get around this issue.

My cozy covers still have a central image in them, but if you look back at the one I showed you in the beginning it's a central image that's so confined to the center of the cover that this edge issue doesn't come into play because most of the cover is a solid color.

I mention this because I want you to be aware of this issue when you do your own cover designs. Hopefully I can help you avoid at least one of the mistakes I have made. (And hopefully more than one by the time we're done here.)

Okay. So let's take that fantasy short story cover we put together earlier and use it to create a print cover.

We're going to do this for KDP paperback, IngramSpark paperback, and IngramSpark hard cover. I always start with the KDP paperback cover, so that's what we'll do here as well.

I am also, so that we have enough spine to work with, going to pretend that this is a full novel we're doing this for.

(If a book is too short there is no spine text allowed as you can actually see on the image above for *Excel for Beginners*. That one, quirkily enough, is at a length that it does have spine text on the IngramSpark version but not on the KDP version.)

First step, we need a template. There is no reason ever for you to create a print cover from absolute scratch. (And also no reason to ever pay for a bar code.)

To get the KDP template, go to the KDP website (https://kdp.amazon.com/en_US/), and click on Help at the top of the screen. In the search bar type, "Create a Paperback Cover" and then click on that help topic. Scroll down on that page that comes up to where there is some blue text that says "cover calculator and template generator," and click on it.

As of right now, that brings up something that looks like this:

Print Cover Calculator and Templates

To find out the exact dimensions of your cover, use the calculator. You can also download a template (PDF and PNG) to be used as a guide layer in your image editing software. Learn more about Hardcover and Paperback cover requirements.

Enter Your Book Information

Binding type

Select one ⌄

Interior type

Select one ⌄

Paper type

Select one ⌄

Page-turn direction

Select one ⌄

Measurement units

Select one ⌄

Interior trim size

Select one ⌄

Page count
Number of pages at your formatted trim size.
Learn more about trim size and page count.

Calculate dimensions

Download Template

Reset book information

I say "as of right now" because this is not what it looked like a year ago and, knowing Amazon, it may not look this way a year from now. They changed all of this when they added hard covers as a print option. Plus, sometimes they just like to change things up so that every guide about how to work with them becomes hopelessly outdated. (Ask me how I know…)

But as long as you know that there are print templates available through their help option you should be able to find and download them. That at least has remained consistent for the last eight or so years.

Anyway. Get to this screen or find the template generator somehow and then tell Amazon what kind of print book you want to create.

You will need to know a few things about your book before you can do this.

First, you need to know how many pages the interior file is going to be. (This means formatted, not just what Word says when you're done. And it includes all front and back matter. So you need the interior done before you can finalize your cover.)

You also need to know what size you want the book to be.

A personal pet peeve of mine is people who use 6 x 9 for paperbacks. I have many, many, many trade published books on my shelves and they are generally not that size in paperback.

In general, for fiction, 6 x 9 is for hard covers. I do have some 6 x 9 fiction paperbacks, but they tend to be either omnibuses—so multiple books in one print edition—or something like a "best of" collection. They are generally not individual titles. The only time I personally use 6 x 9 is for my large print titles.

Also, if you're self-publishing you're probably not creating a mass market title either, which is the smaller print size you can find in bookstores.

What you are likely going to be creating is a trade paperback, which is the larger paperback size that so many books come in these days. So you're looking in the five-inch range not the four- or six- inch range.

If you want to fit in on the shelves with other print books in your genre then go to the library or go to the bookstore and measure some books. (Or bring a bunch of books up on Amazon and look for their print measurements there.)

I personally use 5.25 x 8 for regular print titles. I know others who use 5.5 x 8.5. This is in inches. KDP does give a millimeters option if you want to go that route and are more used to those measurements because you're not in the U.S. so where you are they use slightly different sizes. (Although I'd keep in mind there where you think you'll sell most of your copies and try to choose a size that works for your target market.)

Also, you need to know what kind of paper you want to use because that will impact how wide the spine of your book is. This can also impact the choices you have for trim size.

On KDP you can choose white or cream paper. IngramSpark also offers a groundwood paper option now.

Unless you're doing some sort of fancy, high-priced edition, you're not going to do color. For POD it just costs too much to be feasible and they don't care if it's just one colored page in your book. Any color other than black and white costs lots to print on demand.

The spine width of the KDP template will change with each increment of ten pages. On IngramSpark they're more exact about it and they go down to the exact page count.

Once you know all of that, enter your information, like so:

Next, click on Calculate Dimensions followed by Download Template. This will download a zip file to your computer that contains a PNG file as well as a PDF. I've always worked with the PDF version.

To be able to open the PDF with Affinity, open the zip file, copy the PDF, and paste it outside of the zip file.

Now you're ready to actually work on your cover in Affinity Publisher.

Open Affinity, close out any pop-ups or welcome screens, and then go to File -> Open and navigate to where you placed the PDF cover template.

Click on the file and then click Open. This will bring up the PDF Options dialogue box:

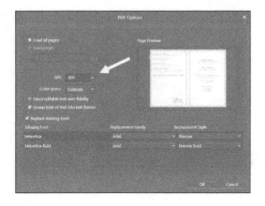

Now. This is key. And it's a mistake I made in GIMP, which is the program I used before this, which screwed up my covers.

You *must* import the PDF file at 300 DPI or more. If you do not do so and you later try to export at 300 DPI, it won't work. You can't fix this after the fact. Garbage in, garbage out.

Also, it won't matter that you added text while you were in the program or that you used a high resolution image, because whatever you import this template at is what will govern all of the elements you put on that cover.

So if you import at 100 DPI, which I think was GIMP's default, that's what all of the elements will be set to. Which will make your spine text blurry at small sizes and your images more muddied.

(Ask me how I know.)

So make sure your DPI value is 300 before you click OK.

Now. The way that Affinity Publisher imports a PDF is it breaks all of the components of the PDF into separate layers. (As opposed to GIMP which imports it as one layer.)

Which means the first thing I do when that file imports is I go to the Layers studio, click on a layer, use Ctrl + A to select all of the layers, and then use Ctrl + G to group them. That reduces all of that noise down to one layer group.

At this point, you should have something that looks like this:

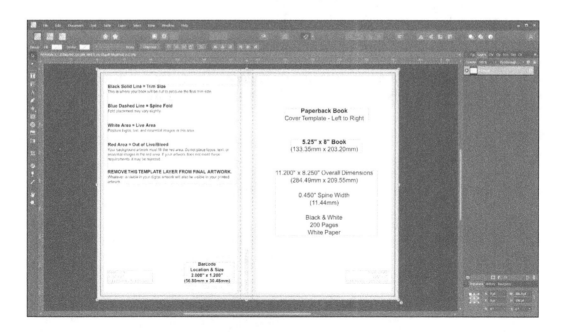

If you want to, you can delete the descriptive text layers from the template. Sometimes I can ignore them, sometimes they annoy me. This time around I'm going to delete them.

To do so, I expand the group I created from the PDF layers, click on the first layer that has a text description (Spine Width…), hold down the shift key and click on the last layer that has a text description (Paperback Book Cover…).

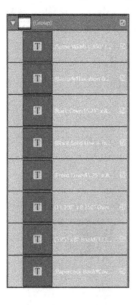

I then use the Delete key which leaves me with just the rectangles that delineate each space. Like so:

Much easier to work with.

My next step is to add the solid-colored background. I'm going to use the fantasy cover we did earlier so I'm going to add a black background.

To do that, I go to the Rectangle Tool on the left-hand side, click and drag to cover the template, and then change the cover to black using the Swatches tab after clicking on the Fill box in the dynamic menu up top.

Remember that it's sometimes easier to add a rectangle by clicking and drawing it within the space first and then dragging each edge to the perimeter of the space. If you have snapping enabled you'll see green or red lines as you do that.

Because I need to see the template for the other layers, I immediately uncheck the box for the rectangle I just added in the Layers studio to hide it for the time being.

Now I can bring in the ebook cover.

The simplest way to do so is to click on the Place Image Tool, navigate to where the cover JPG I created is stored, and then click and drag on the white space on the right-hand side to place the cover.

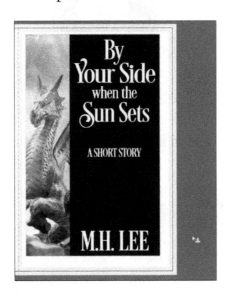

It is not going to fit perfectly.

Place it in as much of the white space as you can manage. Given the cover dimensions I used and the print size I chose, I can fit my cover in the white space with just a little bit of white showing on the left- and right-hand sides.

Keep the cover within the white space because this is the space that is guaranteed to print. The pink space on the right edge and top and bottom is what may or may not print. The pink space on the left edge may end up on the spine.

That's the quick and dirty way to do this. The advantage is that you don't have to mess with each individual item that was on the ebook cover. They're all set where they need to be compared to one another.

But the disadvantage is that I'm going to have a black border on the left of the dragon image and at the top and bottom.

It'll look something like this:

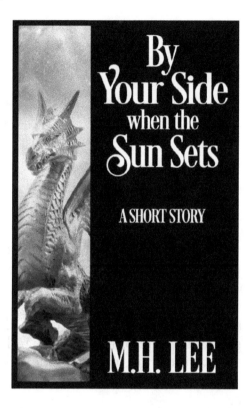

Which is fine. I'm generally okay with that and would probably do this cover that way.

But you may not be.

If you aren't, then what you need to do is bring in the cover elements separately. So delete the layer with the ebook cover that we just created here for our print file, and then go and open the Affinity Publisher file for the ebook cover.

Note, this is the Affinity Publisher file not the JPG file.

In that file, select all of the layers except for Master A and your background. Copy them using Ctrl + C. Click over to your print template and paste them using Ctrl + V. It'll look something like this:

(If you don't like that you can also copy in the background so all of the elements are more visible when you paste them in. It can just cause issues later if you ever change the background for the print book because you'll also have this background layer for the front cover section that's separate and will also need to be changed.)

When you pasted in the layers from the ebook cover, they will still be grouped together. And will also generally paste onto the left-hand side of the template.

Left-click and drag to move the entire group to the right-hand white space for the front cover. You may also need to resize the grouped layers from the corner to fit them into the space.

Also, make sure the layers pasted in above your background layer. If not, go to the Layers studio and move the group or the background layer so that the background layers is lower.

You can always turn on the rectangle layer to see how white text that's not currently showing well will look:

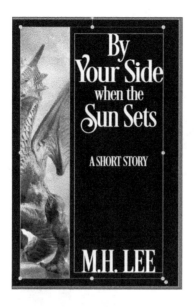

The problem now is the need to work with white text on a white background while making sure that the individual elements stay in good alignment with one another and the template.

I want to see the elements in the template that are behind my black background, but I also want to see the text I'm working with.

What I can do is click on the black rectangle layer in the Layers studio, make sure it's checked so it's visible, but change its opacity to about 70%. I've done that here:

Note how I can now see the white text and also see the template parameters?

I'll need to change this opacity setting back at the end, but this lets me work with my white text and the template at the same time.

The reason we did all of this was to extend the picture frame for the image on the front cover. So let's click on that picture frame in the Layers studio and then go to the canvas and extend the frame all the way to the top and bottom edge of the template. Let's also extend it to the dotted line along the spine.

After I do that I also need to reposition my image in the frame.

That gives me a cover that will look something like this:

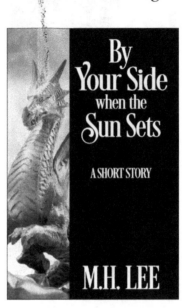

This is print on demand, so it's not guaranteed that I won't have a little bit of black creeping around the edge of the spine there, but at least I won't have to worry about uneven top and bottom edges if I do it this way.

We're not going to do it here, but if I had the right kind of image I could actually have that image wrap around the spine and extend all the way to the back edge of the print cover. That's the only guaranteed way to not have any problems with the image and the spine.

Problem is, though, I'd then have spine text on the image and I'd probably need to use some more advanced tricks to make my spine text and back cover copy visible over that image.

And no matter what you do with POD printing you'll always have some variance somewhere.

So we're just going with black spine and black back cover and doing the best we can.

Which means the next step we have is to add our back cover copy. Click on the Frame Text Tool and then click and drag on the white space for the back cover to create a box where you can place your back cover copy.

I don't take the text frame to the edges of the space, which means I try to place my text frame so that it's centered in the white space on the back cover and has an equal amount of white on the left and right sides.

Again, this is POD so there's going to be some variance each time the cover prints so even if you get it perfectly centered there is no guarantee it will print that way every time.

Once the text frame is in position, click on the Artistic Text Tool and then into the frame and add your back cover copy. I copied mine from a Word document so it pasted in black and in Arial 11.2 pt. Which meant the next step was to select all (Ctrl + A) and change the font, font color, and font size.

I also decided to center my text because there wasn't a lot of it. I would've liked to bold and italicize the top line, but because I was using the Desire font I didn't have those weight options to work with.

But here it is:

You can obviously get more fancy with your back cover. You can put in an author photo and bio, for example. Or a review blurb or two. Whatever you want to put there. For text, I recommend using the text frames. For photos I'd use the Picture Frame Rectangle Tool.

On the KDP template you do not need to include a bar code, they put it in there for you. That yellow rectangle on the template marks where it will go. Don't put anything important in that space. It's fine if your background image goes across that space, but they'll reject the cover if your author bio or something like that encroaches on that space.

Next up and the final element is the spine text.

This one I do not use a text frame for, although you could.

I just click on the Artistic Text Tool and then click on or about the spine and type in the title.

(You may need to click and drag to create an A before you can start typing. That just happened to me, but it doesn't always so it could've been down to whatever tool I had selected just beforehand.)

I try to keep my spine text in all caps because it makes positioning the text in the center of the spine easier.

My text was in Arial and in black so I needed to select all and change that as well.

Next, I need to rotate the text so it fits on the spine.

To do so, go to Layer->Transform->Rotate Right. That should rotate your text to vertical with the tops of the letters on the right. (If you were doing a book in Spanish or other languages where spine text faces the other way, you'd want to go the other direction.)

Click and drag the text layer back to the spine.

It needs to fit within the white space on the spine. In my case the text was too big, so I had to select all of the text and change the font size.

It's a good idea to leave a little bit of white space on both sides of your text, because, again, POD variation is going to potentially shift things about a little bit and if you're right up against the margins that may cause your spine text to look really awkward. (I don't think it would actually wrap around to the front or back cover, but it would probably go right up to the edge.)

When you upload the template you'll also see that Amazon's review page has very bright red lines showing where you cannot have spine text.

Okay.

Once the text is the right size, you can move that layer to the position along the spine that you want.

I tend to put my title towards the top and my author name towards the bottom. If you have a series, try to position your text starting at the same spot on each cover so that they line up nicely on the shelf.

(Another one I have messed up in the past. But looking at my shelves, I'm not alone in that.)

Once you position the title, you can right-click on that layer in the Layers studio and Duplicate, then click into the canvas and drag it down to about where you want your author name.

Make sure the text tool is selected and then click onto the dragged-down layer and replace the text with the author name. Adjust your positioning as needed.

Since the KDP template has nothing added outside of the cover itself (unlike IngramSpark, which we'll see in a minute) you can have Affinity center your spine text for you. Just click on each layer and use the Align Center, Align Horizontally menu option at the very top.

At this point it's a good idea to check that you don't have a bottom-heavy font or a font that in some way doesn't easily center. To do that, zoom in on your spine text. (View->Zoom->400%)

This one looks pretty good to me. If it didn't, I'd either manually adjust or choose a different font.

Zoom the view back (View->Zoom->Zoom to Width or sometimes Zoom to Fit), change the rectangle layer to 100% opacity, and that should be it.

At this point you could delete the group that has the template layers in it, but since they're completely covered by the background layer we added, you don't have to.

I tend not to because if I want to make tweaks later I want those template layers there to guide me.

Next step is to export as a PDF. Go to File->Export and choose the PDF option.

For KDP you need to be able to export *with bleed* or you'll get an error message that the file isn't the right size.

The "PDF (press ready)" option lets you do this, so select it from the dropdown men. Also make sure that the DPI is set to a minimum of 300.

For a cover you want the whole document. And I usually check to preview when complete.

And here is our final cover PDF:

A basic print cover with the ebook cover image (adjusted in this case to remove a top or bottom black border possibility), spine text with the title and author name, and basic back cover copy.

Keep in mind that if this were a real short story cover the template wouldn't have shown a white space on the spine because for short books (under about 110 pages) Amazon doesn't allow spine text. The white space in each template is all that you have to work with for placing your key elements, so if there isn't white space you can't add text to the spine.

Okay. Now on to IngramSpark covers.

INGRAMSPARK PAPERBACK COVER

Next up is taking the print cover we just created and turning it into an IngramSpark (IS) paperback cover.

This needs to be a separate step because the template that IS uses is different from the KDP template. And there are slight differences in terms of spine width between the two platforms so the covers are not in fact interchangeable.

But it doesn't take too long.

First thing is to get your IS template. Go to the IngramSpark Cover Template Generator, currently found at https://myaccount.ingramspark.com/Portal/Tools/CoverTemplateGenerator and input your information.

If you have already set up your book on IS through to the upload step then most of this information will automatically populate for you when you input the ISBN.

But if you haven't yet, you'll have to manually enter it.

The file type I select is PDF.

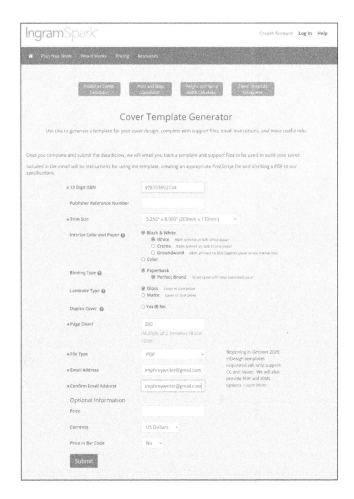

I used to include price in the bar code because as a former bookstore employee I'm used to being able to quickly glance at the bar code on a book and see the price there. But since IS has become a lot more tight-fisted about update codes and has started raising their prices on a more regular basis in the last year, I think I'm probably going to stop doing that. Most of my sales are online anyway.

So fill the form out, hit submit, and you should receive an email with the PDF in it within a few minutes.

You do have to have a valid ISBN for them to generate the template. Above I tried to just make one up and it gave me an error message.

So for this next step I'm going to actually use a template I already have that was for a two-hundred-page book. The concept of what we're about to do won't change if I use an old file. It's just the ISBN on the template that's going to be different.

First step, as before, is to open the PDF file in Affinity, making sure that under PDF Options it's coming in as a 300 DPI image.

(I should note here that I always have it estimate the color space, but if you're doing something fancy with your covers then you should probably set that to CMYK.)

This is what a typical paperback template from IngramSpark looks like:

Note how the actual cover portion is just part of the template. And in this case, the areas where you can put key text and images is pink and the areas that may get cut off or caught on the edge of the spine are blue.

You can also see that the template comes with a bar code on the back cover. This is why you never need to pay for one, because you can always generate an IngramSpark template and use the bar code from there. The bar code is specific to the ISBN you provided.

Below the image it shows the trim size of the book, the details about the book formatting like page count, and the book ISBN. They will reject a cover file that has the wrong ISBN on it.

If you change any of the information you can see on this template, you need to generate a new template and create a new cover. And if you have already published the book and change the title, author, type of paper, or interior color that requires a new ISBN.

Okay. So getting back to the cover design.

The first thing I do when I import the IS template is I group all of the PDF layers. Just like we did with the KDP template. So Layers studio, click on a layer, Ctrl + A, Ctrl + G.

Next I turn the bar code layers into their own group.

The nice thing is that the bar code is the first three layers in the template. So expand that group you just created in the Layers studio, select the first three layers (using Shift or Ctrl to select multiple layers at once), and then use Ctrl + G to group those first three layers into their own subgroup.

Next, left-click and drag that bar code group you just created above the larger group that has all of the PDF layers. Like so:

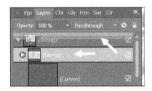

You'll still need to drag the bar code group above the background layer in a minute for it to be visible, but this at least gets it into its own separate layer where you can be reminded to do that. (And if you forget, which I do on occasion, IngramSpark seems to add one for you. I know there are times I've forgotten but the proof showed a bar code.)

Now that we're done with getting the template sorted, we're ready to bring in all of the elements we used for the KDP cover.

Open the KDP cover Affinity file and select all of the layers except the Group layer you created of the KDP PDF template. Ctrl + C to copy, click back over to the IS template, and Ctrl + V to paste.

As it did with the ebook cover when we pasted that in, Affinity tends to paste things to the top left corner by default.

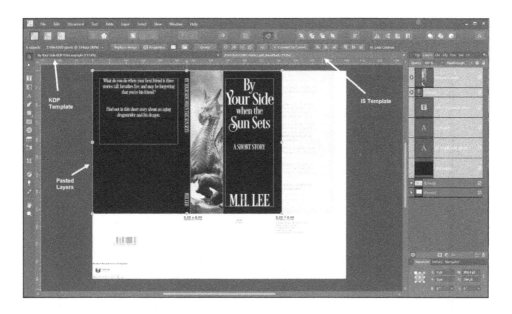

Everything will still be grouped at this point, so you can easily left-click and drag the group over to cover the section of the IS template that is meant for the cover.

I try to drag the cover into place so that the top and at least one side show my alignment lines as you can see here with this close-up of the top left corner where I have both a green and a red alignment line showing:

That may be hard to see in print. My apologies.

At this point I click onto the Rectangle layer in the Layers studio so that I'm only dealing with my background layer, and I click and drag from each side and from the top and bottom to make sure that my background is covering the area on the template devoted to the cover.

So I will either click and drag out and back in or in and back out until I see those red or green lines.

It's a bit redundant since I'd already lined up two sides. I could have just done the other two sides and been fine, but I do it that way anyway.

And, actually, the KDP and IS templates should be the same size top to bottom, it's the width that's slightly different. But still.

Okay. Next step is to hide that layer. So click on the box next to the Rectangle layer in the Layers studio. Your canvas should now look something like this:

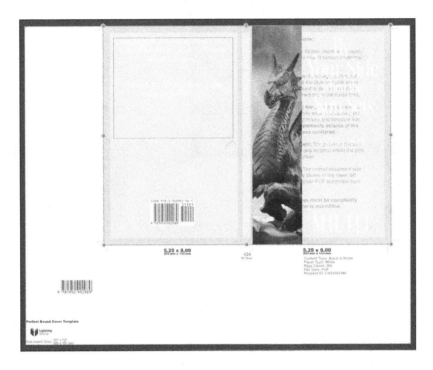

What you're looking for here is that the back cover copy is still centered, that the spine text is centered, and that the front cover elements still fall in the main cover space without issue or need for adjustment.

You will almost always need to adjust the spine text.

Often I have to adjust the back cover copy frame. This time it looks okay, though. Maybe it could go a smidge to the right.

If I want to be exact, there's a layers trick I can use with the IS template that doesn't work with the KDP template. And that's to pull up a specific layer from the PDF template elements to right below the layer I'm trying to place. This lets me see the distance for the layer I'm trying to place compared to that portion of the template.

(If you don't do this you'll notice that Affinity gives you a distance but it's not always to where you want. It might be to the edge of the template instead of the edge of the pink space on the back cover, for example.)

Let's do this for the spine text.

First step. Go to the group for the PDF template and expand it and then scroll down until you find the thin pink vertical layer that represents the spine text.

Click on that layer and then go to the gray and yellow square images in the topmost area of the workspace and find the one that says "Move to Front":

Click on that and it should move the spine layer up to the top of the group. You can then easily click and move it the rest of the way up to just below the spine text layer.

Here is the Layers studio with it moved up to just below the title and author name layers for the spine:

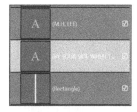

Next step is to Zoom in to 400% or so and then move around until you can see the title on the spine. Here we can clearly see that the title is no longer centered:

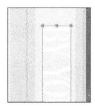

But Affinity can't center this for us against the overall template like it did for the KDP template, because the cover on the template is not centered. What we can do, though, is click on the title layer and use the left and right arrows to move the title until the values showing on the right and left-hand side of the title are the same.

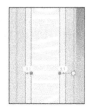

Because we moved the pink spine area up right below our title and author layers, the distance that's being shown by Affinity is the distance to the edges of the pink spine area. If we hadn't move that up it would be using different reference points on the left and right sides that were not equidistant from the spine.

You can either do the same thing for the author name or you can use the Transform studio to give that layer the same X value as the title layer.

Zoom back out and move the pink spine layer back below the background layer. It doesn't have to return to where you found it, just move it so that it's no longer visible in your final document.

While you're in the Layers studio, drag the bar code group layer up above the background layer and then go to your workspace and position the bar code where you want it. I usually place it in the bottom right corner of the back cover, so I drag it over and down a bit.

Finally, click on the checkbox for the background layer in the Layers studio to turn it back on.

And that should be it. You should now have your IS paperback cover ready to go.

Export as PDF. This time as PDF/X-1a:2003, which seems to work with IS. You want the whole document but you do not need to include bleed this time around.

And this is what you upload to IngramSpark, extra white space, text, and all.

When you get back your print proof from IS, though, do be sure to zoom in on the PDF file to check your text on your spine.

You can see the dotted lines that extend down from the spine. You want to make sure that no text falls outside of those lines.

Also, be sure there's no blue from the template peeking through along the edges of your image. A pixel worth or so is probably going to be fine, but too much and you run the risk that print variance will sometimes put a white trim along the edge of your cover.

(Even when you get this right, that can still happen if it's a bad print run.)

Okay. One more cover to go, the IngramSpark case laminate hard cover version. It requires more work, but is much the same as what we just did for the paperback.

INGRAMSPARK CASE LAMINATE HARD COVER

The first step is to go back to the cover template generator on the IS website and generate your cover template.

The type of cover we're doing here is a case laminate cover, which means that there is no removable wraparound cover. It prints directly onto the binding just like a paperback cover does.

Unfortunately, perhaps, for hard cover you can't use the same size we just used, it's not available. So this time around we're going to work with a 6 x 9 cover.

So get your template and open it just like we've done before. And make sure it comes in at 300 DPI.

This is what it looks like:

Notice that there is a wider blue border around the edge than for the paperback. Also, the blue space along the spine is much wider. Which is why even if you did your paperback in a 6 x 9 format, too, you'd still have a lot of moving pieces around to make this one work.

Also notice that the cover itself is positioned differently from the positioning of a paperback cover. Less of an issue when working in Affinity, but a big hassle for me when I used to work in GIMP.

First things first, go the Layers studio, select all, and group. (Ctrl + A, Ctrl + G)

Expand that group, take the first three layers and group them into their own subgroup. Move them above the larger group.

Click and drag the bar code that was created from that grouping to where you want it on the canvas. I put mine in the bottom right corner of the back cover.

Next, open your KDP print file or your IS paperback file. Select all but the group layer for the PDF template and the bar code, if applicable, copy (Ctrl + C), go back to your IS case laminate template, and paste (Ctrl + V).

Click and drag the group into place as best you can, but they're not going to fit because of the extra space the case laminate cover requires along the spine.

It's a starting point, though:

I've lined the cover up as best I can along the spine, but you can see there's a lot of extra space around the edges. This I partially because I'm moving from a 5.25 x 8 cover to a 6 x 9 cover but also because of the difference between a case laminate hard cover and a paperback cover.

Now that we have the layers generally where they need to be we can go through each one and make our necessary adjustments.

First up, the background layer. Click on it in the Layers studio to select just it and then go back to the canvas and drag from each edge to the edges of the blue perimeter for the cover.

You should see the green and red lines along the perimeter if you've matched it up with the cover template underneath.

Hide that layer once you're done with it.

Now you can see how the other layers also need to be moved around:

The spine text will need some adjustment, too, but since I placed the layers along the spine it's not off by near as much.

I'm going to start with the back cover copy. I click on that layer in the Layers studio to select it and then click on that text frame in the workspace and drag it over. One nice thing with this particular template is that Affinity will show when it's centered in the pink active area with a green line through the middle, so no guessing or having to move things around to see measurements.

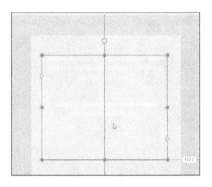

Next up is the cover text and cover image. We can select both of those at once in the Layers studio and move them to the right until the cover image and text are in the pink space and not overlapping the blue area.

Also, I'm going to use the Transform studio here to resize everything so that I don't skew the text or the image.

I need to be careful here that the Lock Aspect Ratio option is turned on. I can confirm that it is when the little interlinking rings are visible on the right-hand side of the W and H value boxes.

Changing the width to 400 pt would give me the width to fill the space, but then the text is pretty close to the edge, so I went with 375. I had to then click and drag to position the image and text evenly within the pink work area:

I now have a few changes to make that are particular to this cover.

See how the image and the author name aren't as far down towards the bottom of the pink space? I want to extend those down. I'm not going to extend the image into the blue areas, I'm okay having a black border on this one and letting it maybe be a little off. But I do at least want it to go as far down on the bottom side as it goes up on the top side.

So I click on the text frame layer and find that the frame is actually the right size. The issue is that the image needs to be moved down.

I expand the text frame layer, click on the image layer, and then click in my workspace and drag the image downward. I think it still works at its current size, so I'll leave it alone in that respect. If it didn't work I'd need to click on the corner and drag or use the Transform studio to resize it to fill the space better.

And if I did do that I'd also need to go to Document->Resource Manager to double-check that my Placed DPI value was still above 300 or I risk having a blurry or smudged printed image.

I also want the author name to drop down a bit as well.

I can click on that layer in the Layers studio and then click on the layer and use the down arrow to move the author name down more.

Be careful with covers that you choose the right layer. I'm inevitably trying to click on the author name from the spine when I need the one from the front cover.

I use the arrow key instead of clicking and dragging so I don't lose my alignment between the author name and the title.

That looks good now:

All that's left is to check on my spine text. It's easiest to do if you zoom in. And as we did before, I usually move the spine text pink space layer up to just below my title and author name layers while I'm working on this.

One other thing to note with case laminate covers is that they do sometimes allow you to use a larger font than you used on the equivalent paperback. It's your call whether you size that text up a bit or not. I'm not going to here.

Zoom back out. Turn on the rectangle layer. Drag the bar code layer above it. Drag the pink spine text layer below the rectangle layer. And you're done.

Because of the excess wraparound for a case laminate cover it can look odd in the template. The best time to really know what it will look like on the front cover at least is in the preview file you get from IngramSpark. (One could wish you saw that before you submit to them, but that's not how their process works. At least at that point you can just go and upload a new cover if needed without paying to do so again.)

And, done. Export as PDF. Same as the other IS cover, I use the PDF/ X-1a:2003 setting.

CONCLUSION

Alright. That's it. We have now covered the basics of creating an ebook cover as well as print covers for IngramSpark and Amazon.

With the tools we covered here you should be able to create perfectly workable covers for most genres. And probably more attractive covers than I create.

The tools are what they are, what you make of them comes down to your design skills, practice, and patience.

Just like with writing, expect to get it wrong the first few times. And to not see that you got it wrong until later. Asking for a friend's opinion and getting silence tells you something. (As much as we'd like to wish it didn't.)

If you do get really serious about cover design, you're probably going to want to buy Affinity Photo and do a lot of your work there. That's where you need to go to work with Photoshop templates, for example. And where you can use layer masks to make text stand out on a busy background.

The good news is that most Photoshop videos and courses can be applied to Affinity Photo. You might have to look up what the tool is called in Affinity or where it's located, but for the most part I've been able to find Photoshop videos and take what I see there and almost immediately apply it in Affinity Photo.

I know that was true at least with the NeoStock videos on cover design where they do some pretty amazing stuff that leaves me in awe of the level of effort and amazing results. Those courses use Photoshop, but the concepts remain the same.

Now, is doing your own covers ideal? No, of course not.

In an ideal world we'd all be able to get immediate access to a top-level cover designer and have the money to burn to pay $500+ for an amazing cover for even the most basic of short stories.

But we don't live in an ideal world. And learning to do your own covers lets you (a) publish things you wouldn't otherwise, (b) pivot quickly, and (c) potentially earn more money.

I'll close with one final thought: Don't be afraid to try and fail. Very often in indie-world you are going to run into people who are very vocal about their judgements. According to them you can't self-edit, you can't make your own covers, you can't publish a novel until you've spent a decade honing your craft, etc. Basically, you're doing it wrong unless you're spending a fortune and an expert before you even begin.

And only if you're making seven figures a year can you possibly argue with them on these points. Of course, if you are making seven figures a year and doing any of that yourself then they'll just say you're an outlier and no one else could do that so they're still right.

But here's the deal.

I know too many authors who had beautiful packaging and failed.

Because what they needed was the type of editing most of us can neither find nor afford. Or they needed to learn about hitting the market. Everything about the book was fine, but the market they wrote for was a hundred people, half of whom don't buy self-published books.

And since they'd "done everything right" they gave up. If they could spend thousands for editing and covers and sell fifty copies then what was the point? So they walked away.

The beauty of doing this yourself is that you can do what my Wharton professor told us in our entrepreneurship class: "fail fast, fail cheap". Or, the corollary, succeed fast and cheap and then fix your mistakes on the fly. You're not locked into anything in this business.

Now, don't get me wrong. I'm not saying put out crap work. I'm saying get it to the point where it's good enough for people to try and then get them to try it without bankrupting yourself in the process. If you have something people like, they'll tell you with their money. They'll buy it. If you don't, they'll tell you with their silence. (Hopefully. Because that's certainly better than getting a bunch of bad reviews or nasty emails.)

Once you have a glimmer that what you've created has potential, then you can see about putting in all of that money.

And, yes, I realize that some will make the chicken and the egg argument here: Without good covers you can't get good sales. But as someone who has put books up with covers I've made myself, I can tell you that you will know when you've hit on something that people are interested in. And if that happens? The best thing to do...

Write more of it. As soon as you can.

You can rebrand later. First, get more product into the hands of the people who already found you and loved you.

Okay. Anyway. I digress and I'm probably preaching to the choir here if you read this far.

So let's close this out.

There is also a video course version of this book available on my Teachable store at https://ml-humphrey.teachable.com/. Use code MLH50 to get fifty percent off the course cost.

Also, if you hadn't already, you might want to check out *Affinity Publisher for Ad Creatives*, which walks you through how to use Affinity Publisher to create ad images for Amazon A+ Content, Facebook ads, Bookbub ads, and more.

Good luck with it. Feel free to reach out if you have questions. Even if I don't know the answer I'm usually pretty good at tracking them down.

APPENDIX A: AFFINITY PUBLISHER QUICK TAKES

BACKGROUND COLOR

ADD

See Rectangle Insert and then Color Apply Specific.

COLOR

APPLY SPECIFIC

To apply a specific color use the Color studio. Double-click on the filled circle or doughnut, whichever is on top, to open the Color Chooser dialogue box. Enter your specific values in the fields for RGB, HSL, CMYK, or the color's hex value next to the # sign. For bright yellow I use FFD500.

CHANGE

For text and fill color there will often be a rounded rectangle in the dynamic menu bar at top showing the current color. Click on that to see a dropdown menu of color choices. The Swatches tab is best for black, white, and shades of gray as well as recent colors used in the document. The Color tab is good for all other solid colors. The eyedropper on the Color tab can be used to choose a color from the canvas. Click on the color swatch you want or into the rectangle of shaded colors in the Color tab to apply. For the eyedropper, double-click on the color next to the eyedropper to apply.

ELEMENTS

CENTER

Layers studio. Select element or elements. Alignment dropdown in top menu. Align Center under Align Horizontally to center left to right or Align Middle under Align Vertically to center top to bottom.

DISTRIBUTE EVENLY

Place left-most and right-most or top-most and bottom-most elements at the outer edge of desired range. Select all elements in the Layers studio.

Alignment dropdown in top menu. Align Horizontally, Space Horizontally to distribute evenly left to right. Align Vertically, Space Vertically to distribute evenly top to bottom.

GROUP AND MOVE

Layers studio. Group layers. Move Tool. Left-click and drag.

GROUP AND RESIZE

Layers studio. Group layers. Click on grouped layers in workspace. Left-click and drag from blue circles around perimeter.

EXPORT

JPG

Go to File and then Export. Choose JPEG at the top of the dialogue box. Set Quality to around 85. Click on Export. Navigate to where you want to export the file. Edit the name if needed. Click on Save.

PDF

Go to File and then Export. Choose PDF. For KDP choose the PDF(press ready) option so that the file exports with bleed. For IngramSpark choose the PDF/X-1a:2003 option. Make sure DPI is 300 or more.

PNG

Go to File and then Export. Choose PNG at the top of the dialogue box. Click on Export. Navigate to where you want to export the file. Edit the name if needed. Click on Save.

FILE

NEW

Ctrl + N or go to File and then New in the top menu. Or you can choose New Document when you open Affinity.

OPEN

Ctrl + O or go to File and then Open. Navigate to the file, click on it, click on Open. For a file that was recently open you can go to File and then Open Recent and choose the file from the secondary dropdown menu.

SAVE

Ctrl + S or go to File and then Save in the top menu. To rename or save the file to a new location go to File and then Save As.

GUIDE LINES

ADD

Left-click and drag from the ruler around the workspace onto the canvas. Dragging from the top will add a horizontal line. Dragging from the left side will add a vertical line.

REMOVE

Left-click and drag the guideline off of the workspace. If you can't select the guideline, make sure that the Move Tool is selected first.

HEART

SHAPE INSERT

Rectangle Tool dropdown. Heart Tool. Left-click and drag on the canvas.

IMAGE

CONVERT TO BLACK AND WHITE

Select image layer in Layers studio. Go to Layer then New Adjustment and Black & White. Or click on the Layer Adjustments half-filled circle at the bottom of the Layers studio and choose Black & White from the dropdown menu there.

FLIP

Select the image layer. Go to Layer, then Transform, and then choose Flip Horizontal or Flip Vertical.

INSERT

Place Image Tool. Select image to insert. Open. Image may automatically insert. If not, click and drag in workspace until desired size.

INSERT IN PICTURE FRAME

Click on picture frame layer. Place Image Tool. Select image to insert. Open. Image will insert in frame.

LOCK ASPECT RATIO

In the Transform studio left-click on the two links with a small bar connecting them to the right side of the fields for the W and H values. If Lock Aspect Ratio is enabled there will be a line that extends from the links and connect them to the two fields. If it is not enabled there will just be the two links.

MOVE

Move Tool. Click in the center of the four arrows in the center of the image if in a picture frame. Or go to the image layer and click directly on the image. Hold left-click and drag to desired location.

REPLACE

Document top menu option. Resource Manager. Select image. Replace. Select new image. Open. Close resource manager.

RESIZE

Move Tool. Click on image layer or directly on image if not in a picture frame. Option A: Transform studio. Lock Aspect Ratio. Change height or width value. Option B: Click on blue circle in corner and drag at an angle to resize proportionately. Or click on blue circle along any edge to change height or width only. This will skew most images.

RESIZE IN PICTURE FRAME

If you are clicked into the picture frame layer there will be a slider below the frame. You can move the slider to the right or left to resize the image in the picture frame.

ROTATE

Select the image layer. Go to Layer, Transform, Rotate Right or Rotate Left. Or go to the Transform studio and enter a value for R. Or left-click on the white filled circle outside the perimeter of the image and hold that left-click as you drag to the right or the left.

SEPIA

Apply Black & White layer adjustment to the image layer. Then go to Layer and Layer Effects or click on the Layer Effects option at the bottom of the Layers studio. Check the box for Color Overlay. Click on the text for Color Overlay. Change Opacity to approximately 50%. Change the color to a darker golden-toned brown color.

LAYER

DELETE

Right-click on the layer in the Layers studio and select Delete from the dropdown menu or click on the layer and use the Delete key.

DUPLICATE

Right-click on the layer in the Layers studio and select Duplicate from the dropdown menu.

GROUP

Select the layers you want to group using the Ctrl key (for layers that are not adjacent) or the Shift key (for layers that are). Left-click on each layer and hold down Shift or Ctrl as you select the rest. Then use Ctrl + G to group the layers or right-click and select Group from the dropdown menu.

HIDE

Uncheck the box next to the layer name in the Layers studio.

MOVE

Left-click and drag a layer up or down to its desired position. The blue shading will show where the layer will go. You can also use the gray and yellow box images in the top menu to move a layer all the way to the top, all the way to the bottom, or up or down one space.

TRANSPARENCY

To change the transparency of a layer, select it in the Layers studio, click on the dropdown for Opacity at the top of the studio, and then adjust the slider to the desired degree of transparency.

UNGROUP

Right-click on the grouped layers in the Layers studio and choose Ungroup from the dropdown menu. Or use Ctrl + Shift + G.

UNHIDE

Check the box next to the layer name in the Layers studio.

NEW DOCUMENT PRESET

ADD

File->Open to start a new document. Make changes in the New Document dialogue box to create a new layout. Click on the + sign next to Custom at the top of the layout settings.

CHOOSE

In the New Document dialogue box click on the preset and then click on Create. Some presets will be under different headings such as Print, Press Ready, etc. and you will need to click on that heading first.

RENAME

Right-click on the thumbnail for the preset. Choose Rename Preset. Type new name. OK.

PICTURE FRAME

BORDER

Select the picture frame layer in the Layers studio. Make sure the Move Tool is selected. To add a border, in the dynamic menu at the top, click on the white line with a red slash through it to the right of Stroke and change the Width value to the desired width. Click on the colored field next to Stroke to change the color of the line. To remove a border, click on the solid line to the right of Stroke in the dynamic menu and then click on the circle with a red slash through the middle next to Style in the dropdown menu.

INSERT

Picture Frame Rectangle Tool. Click and drag to place picture frame on canvas.

MOVE

Select the picture frame layer in the Layers studio. If the Move Tool is selected, left-click anywhere on the frame in the workspace and drag. If the Text Tool is selected, left-click on the perimeter of the frame and drag. Or use the Transform studio to provide a specific X or Y value.

RESIZE

Select the picture frame layer in the Layers studio. Left-click and drag from any of the blue circles around the perimeter of the frame.

RESIZE FRAME AND IMAGE SIMULTANEOUSLY

Select the picture frame layer in the Layers studio. Left-click and drag from the blue circle outside of the perimeter of the frame in the bottom right corner.

RECTANGLE

ANGLE

Select the layer for the rectangle in the Layers studio. Go to the Transform studio and change the S value.

INSERT

Rectangle Tool. Left-click and drag on the canvas.

SELECT ALL

SELECT ALL

Ctrl + A.

SNAPPING

ENABLE

Go to the horseshoe shaped magnet image in the top center of the top menu. Click on the dropdown arrow. Check the box next to Enable Snapping.

STAR

SHAPE INSERT

Rectangle Tool dropdown. Star Tool. Left-click and drag on the canvas.

TEXT INSERT

Artistic Text Tool. Glyph Browser. Wingdings font. Double-click on star shape.

STUDIO

ANCHOR

Left-click on studio and drag to the left or right-hand side of the workspace until you see a blue outline appear and then release. To move within a series of tabs, simply left-click and drag.

CLOSE

Go to View and then Studio and select the name of the studio you want to close. Or, left-click on the studio, drag it away from the workspace so that it is a standalone dialogue box, and click on the top right corner to close it.

MOVE

Left-click on studio dialogue box or tab and drag to move to desired location.

OPEN

Go to View and then Studio and select the studio you want.

STUDIO PRESET

ADD NEW

Arrange studios as desired. Go to View in top menu. Then Studio Presets. Add Preset. Type name. OK.

APPLY

Option 1: Go to View in top menu and then Studio Presets and select desired preset. Option 2: Ctrl + Shift + [Number] for the desired preset.

DELETE

Go to View in top menu. Then Studio Presets and Manage Studio Presets. Select preset name. Delete. Close.

RENAME

Go to View in top menu. Then Studio Presets and Manage Studio Presets. Select preset name. Rename. Type in new name. OK. Close.

RESET

To reset to the original studio preset go to View and then Studio and Reset Studio.

SAVE CHANGES

Make desired changes to studio preset arrangement. Go to View in top menu. Then Studio Presets. Add Preset. Type in exact same name as before. OK. Agree to overwrite old preset when prompted.

TEXT

ADD

To add text directly onto your canvas, select the Artistic Text Tool, and then click on the canvas and type. You may need to left-click on the canvas and drag to form an A before you can type.

ADD SPECIAL SYMBOLS OR CHARACTERS

Artistic Text Tool. Click into workspace where desired. Go to the Glyph Browser. Find desired symbol or character. Double-click on symbol or character to insert.

ALIGNMENT (LEFT TO RIGHT)

Artistic Text Tool. Click on the text layer. Go to the menu choices in the dynamic menu above the workspace. There are four images with lines. Align Left, Align Center, Align Right, or use the dropdown menu for Justify Left, Justify Center, Justify Right, Justify All, Align Towards Spine, Align Away From Spine.

ALIGNMENT (TOP TO BOTTOM)

Artistic Text Tool. Click on the text layer. Go to the menu choices in the dynamic menu above the workspace. Use the dropdown menu for Top Align, Center Vertically, Bottom Align, or Justify Vertically.

ALL CAPS OR SMALL CAPS

Artistic Text Tool. Select the text to be formatted. Go to Character studio. Typography section. Click on the two capital Ts (TT) to apply all caps. Click on the capital T with a lowercase T (Tt) to apply small caps.

FONT

Artistic Text Tool. Select text. Dynamic menu at top, left-hand side. Font dropdown. Choose font. Or select text and go to Character studio font dropdown at top.

LINE SPACING (LEADING)

Artistic Text Tool. Select paragraph. Paragraph studio. Spacing section. Change value in Leading dropdown. Default is usually a good place to start. With design work it's often better to just have each line of text as its own layer so you can manually adjust the spacing between elements.

ROTATE

Select the layer with the text you want to rotate and then change the R value in the Transform studio. You can also left-click and drag the white circle outside the edge of the text layer from the canvas itself.

SIZE

Artistic Text Tool. Select text. Dynamic menu at top, left-hand side. Font size dropdown. Choose size or type in size. Or select text and go to Character studio font size dropdown at top.

WEIGHT

Artistic Text Tool. Select text. Dynamic menu at top, left-hand side. Font weight dropdown. (Will usually default to Regular.) Choose from available weights for that font. Or select text and go to Character studio font weight dropdown at top.

TEXT FRAME

ALIGN OR POSITION

Frame Text Tool or Move Tool. Left-click on text frame and hold as you drag. Look for red and green alignment lines to center or align to other elements in workspace. (Turn on Snapping if there are no red or green lines.) Use Alignment dropdown in top menu to align to workspace, not the dynamic menu bar that applies to actual text.

INSERT

Frame Text Tool on left-hand side. Click and drag in workspace.

RESIZE

Click on text frame layer. Left-click and drag on one of the blue circles around the perimeter of the text. Click and drag at an angle from the corner to keep scaling proportionate.

UNDO

Ctrl + Z. Or you can open the History studio and rewind using the slider or by clicking back onto a prior step.

INDEX

ABOUT THE AUTHOR

M.L. Humphrey is a self-published author with both fiction and non-fiction titles published under a variety of pen names. When she gets stuck on her next fiction project she foolishly decides to write books that only ten people are going to buy, although she does usually learn something interesting in the process so it's worth it in the end.

You can reach her at:

mlhumphreywriter@gmail.com

or at

www.mlhumphrey.com